SUPER

SUPER

THE AUTOBIOGRAPHY OF
SCOTT DIXON

First published by Pitch Publishing, 2019

Pitch Publishing
A2 Yeoman Gate
Yeoman Way
Worthing
Sussex
BN13 3QZ
www.pitchpublishing.co.uk
info@pitchpublishing.co.uk

ISBN 978 1 78531 519 0

Typesetting and origination by Pitch Publishing
Printed and bound in India by Replika Press Pvt. Ltd.

Contents

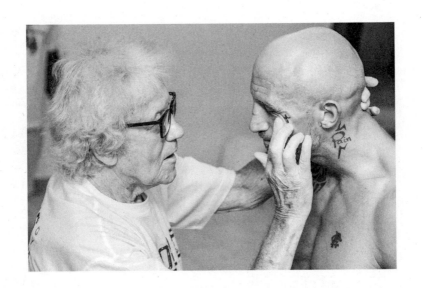

Dedication

I dedicate this book to my grandfather,
Toby Dixon, forever my Papa. A tough
act to follow, he not only cared for me in
countless ways throughout my life, but
also told me something I will never forget:
'A real man goes home to his family
after a day's work.'

Introduction

The story you're about to read is truly amazing – and incredibly all factual. Scott Dixon's story has been described as 'a real *Rocky* story', but I don't believe this description does it justice. There is just no tale quite like this. As a boxing fan, I had been aware of Scott Dixon for a few years, but it was only after digging deep before his world title win in 2012 that I discovered what a dramatic life he had led.

The Hamilton fighter will admit that he's no saint, but he didn't deserve the kind of awful dramas that came his way. As a kid, he always wanted to fight, but becoming world champion was something he could only dream about. Scott has been fighting ever since he could put one foot in front of another, due to the encouragement of his grandfather and renowned Newarthill boxing coach, Toby Dixon.

Scott was just eight years old, the age at which most children played with teddy bears and tiddlywinks, when he first stepped between the ropes. After a brief time as an amateur fighter, Scott quickly turned pro in 1995 at the age of 19. After 16 wins and two draws, Scott was tipped for the very top in 1998 before tasting defeat to Michael Carruth on points in Dublin.

Two years later, after winning the World Boxing Board, Commonweath and Scottish welterweight titles, as well as suffering defeats in high-profile fights against Anthony Farnell, Mehrdud Takaloo, Steve Roberts and Derek Roche, Scott won the WBU international light-middleweight title by knocking out unbeaten local Manchester hero Jamie Moore in 2000, proving he was still a fighter to be reckoned with.

Unlike many stars in boxing today, Scott wasn't afraid to fight anybody, anywhere. But tragically, after a violent incident in 2004, he had no choice but to hang up his gloves. It looked to be the end of Scott's boxing story. The 27-year-old Scot was abducted from his house in Hamilton, viciously attacked, shot, stabbed, beaten with a hammer, driven to the countryside and left to die.

Not surprisingly, with a metal plate in his arm and other lasting physical and mental scars from the attack, Scott wasn't seen in the ring again for quite some time. Fearing his career was over, Scott took to drink and drugs and, at his lowest ebb, contemplated taking his own life, but through sheer grit and determination, he returned to boxing in 2007.

When you read Scott's story, you don't know whether to laugh or cry. At times, his life in the murk and violence of criminal underworlds is shocking and as the story gradually unfolds, you understand that the real battle is being fought internally with Scott – between hope and despair.

Scott Dixon, who was Brad Pitt's body-double in the movie *Snatch*, portraying an unbeatable street boxer, and well known for his Superman shorts and theme music, depicting a superhuman athlete, still chokes up when he thinks back to the brutal attack that left him unable to walk for 18 months.

Through it all, in August 2012, Scott completed a fairytale comeback by winning the German version of the WBU super-middleweight title, outpointing Baker Barakat over 12 rounds. Eight years after Scott was brutally beaten, 83-year-old Toby Dixon flew to Malta to watch Scott use the skills he'd learned, as a child and throughout his life, and succeed as a professional boxer and man.

Scott is now enjoying life in Malta but still wants to return to the place of his birth, Scotland. Away from the gym, he is a full-time father and dotes on his young son, Toby, named after his grandfather. To understand the impact of Dixon's gripping story, readers should listen to those familiar with it.

'Scott is a great fighter, and he deserves every success after what he's been through,' said Oscar De La Hoya. Alex Morrison, the godfather of Scottish boxing, added, 'He has been through an awful lot, so he has done incredibly well. Scott is a smashing guy and a great fella. He deserves everything good that comes his way.' While his story is anything but a fictional drama, maybe Big Joe Egan was right when he summed up Dixon's life as a 'real, true-to-life *Rocky* story', describing Scott as 'a true fighting warrior'.

Chris Roberts, late sports reporter for the *Daily Record*.

Round 1

Ambushed

18 May 2004

I was in high spirits, feeling prosperous. I'd just fought an Irish fella, Matthew Macklin, who was known as The Tipperary Tornado. All boxers enjoyed pumped-up, flashy and nonsensical names like that. I was no exception. It was just a bit of a noise to capture the attention of supporters and newspapers. I had fought him six days earlier at the Rivermead Leisure Centre in Reading but could still feel it throughout my body. I'd taken a bit of a hammering, but so had he. A lot of my straight lefts, peachy rights and uppercuts had got through his defences. Not enough to get the better of him, drop him or finish him, but the fight had a good turnout. Whatever the result, with 2,000 people in attendance, it wasn't a bad payday.

New kid on the block and much-fancied, Macklin was trained by Billy Graham, who also had Ricky Hatton in his stable. Macklin was a British-born Irishman. He was on a roll and heading for the dazzling, bright lights of success. He hadn't been flattened, so far as I knew. I was beaten but it was a good enough performance. 'Not enough time to prepare' was beginning to sound like the story of my life. I was in reasonable shape and my mind was focused sharp like a camera with a zoom lens, but it wasn't enough.

In boxing, a lot of opportunities come late in the day. You grab them if the price is right, or you leave them. I never turned down work. You never knew if there was going to be more work, and I grew up in a place where work was scarce. Also, I'm a bit of a chancer. If opportunity knocked on my door, I usually answered. Somebody drops out, somebody steps in. No promoter ever wanted to cancel a fight. It's bad for business and reputations. There was always someone else up for it, whether it was a fall guy or someone trying to get their career off the mat. Guys who try to make a comeback rarely do. That's sad to say, but it's also true. Just look at the evidence. I usually answered the door.

So, I got a crack at Macklin and held my head up. I didn't get floored. Floored meant you held your head down and wondered after a loss, 'What next? Should I just pack it all in?' I just stashed the experience away in my boxing memory bank for the next time. There *would* be a next time. I hadn't been floored.

Today was a familiar clockwork routine. I untangled myself from a bird I'd met the night before at a nearby club called The Ritz. It was hardly a flashy spot like The Ritz in London, but a very different Hamilton, Scotland variety of ritzy. I asked her, whatever her name was, to let herself out. After she left, I hauled myself out of bed and went to Alex Morrison's gym on Swanston Street for a quick shave, wash and a shower. I used his gym regularly when I was in Glasgow. It wasn't too far from Hamilton, where I grew up. The gym was a massive, vibrant place with four rings, top-notch gear, a changing room and showers.

Frequented by up-and-coming boxers and worn-out punch-drunks with nothing else to do, the gym was always packed to the rafters, reeking of sweat and fear. Today, two top Rangers boys who I followed, Barry Ferguson and Gordon Smith, were working out. They were my football heroes. Another character known as 'Nicker' Harris, who couldn't hurt a fly and was as skinny as Olive Oyl, was hanging around, too. The Invisible Man we called him, which suited his trade.

Like clockwork, first of December, he'd turn up with a scrap of paper and a Biro to take down festive orders: whisky, gin, brandy, Drambuie, Baileys for the birds, ale and fags. We're talking cases of it. Then 'poof', Nicker would vanish and go bust a warehouse. He made enough money in a month to keep him afloat all year, a truly seasonal businessman: 11 months off, one month on. After filling his orders, he would head to Spain and put his feet up. It was odd to see him here in May. Someone once asked him how he got all his stuff. He ran his finger down his nose, closed his eyes and whispered, 'Magic.'

Up-and-coming celebrities worked out here, too. All up, the gym had a hotchpotch gathering of all sorts and was very much the place to be and be seen. There were pros, promoters, trainers, talent scouts, sparring partners, amateurs, teenagers, hopefuls, the hopeless, has-beens, hangers-on and, of course, plenty of tarts and bad apples.

Boxing and crime are like Siamese twins. You don't get one without the other one whispering in your ear. Everybody knew everybody and we all got on or gave each other space. It was a mingling of respectful mistrust, but not everyone followed the fundamental rules of loyalty and silence.

After training, I strolled over to the café next door. It was a regular hustle-bustle hangout. You could get a slice of toast, a cuppa, a cooked breakfast, and a head full of rabbit about who or what was going down. Redhead Janice Tool ran the café with a rod of iron and a rolling pin. She'd take no lip. If anyone said 'boo' to her, they'd have us lot coming down on them. Janice was untouchable.

After breakfast, I left the gym in my new silver Lexus, juiced the car down the road and drove the three miles to see my hairdresser friend, Leanne, at her flat. On the way, I heard on the radio that more rain had fallen in Scotland this past May than in recorded history. Today, we would have a brief respite with sunny spells, then thunderstorms and rain were coming our way. It was a bleak prospect. Already, I felt something wasn't hanging quite right today and I couldn't figure it out.

Maybe it was just the weather: dead depressing. Dark clouds were amassing like upturned mushrooms – fungi gathering in a dank forest and painting over little patches of suspiciously promising blue skies. A strong wind from the east was shilly-shallying and kicking empty beer cans, supermarket plastic bags, fag packets, and discarded rubbish across the road. Everything was already sleeked and greased from the last downpour. Trying to shake all the muck and shit that I saw through my windscreen, my mind drifted to Leanne.

'You're Real Madrid, babe, the one to play for,' I first said to her when we met, fancying the pants straight off her. She was in a league of her own, though. She told me straight what she thought of me.

'You're one big cocky shit,' she replied slyly. I was the moth, and she was the flame. Or, maybe it was the other way around. Lately, I had been thinking about maybe giving it a go with her, but I'm not in the best shape. When I go to the flat, she asks me to sit down on a chair in front of a large mirror, just like a proper hairdresser. I liked that a lot. I could talk to her reflection. I didn't have much hair to cut, so a blow dry was a waste of electricity.

'Whoever's been doing your hair has made a right proper mess of it,' she said with a huff. 'Honestly. It's ginger. If you want blonde, see me,' she added, drying my head with a towel. Getting her to do my hair regular was nothing more than an excuse to see her in private, with ivory-coloured curtains closed around us. She always looked as well turned out as her pad, spotlessly clean and well decorated. She also had a massive telly.

She had framed photos of her family and fast cars – supercharged rally beasts covered in sponsor decals – all neatly displayed on one shelf. She likes to go as fast as she can, I thought. There was even a framed snap of her in racing gear with a crash helmet on behind the wheel of a car. It was all honky-tonk, a picture built to do the business. Just like her.

Leanne was as bonny as they get and funny, all rolled up into one tasty package of fun and games. When she cracked a smile, so did you. Every guy fancied the pants off her, but she was selective. Not everyone can pull that trick off. She had lovely ice-blue eyes and proper blonde hair with no dark roots and none of that filthy ammonia-stinking bleach shit that gets up your nose. If she'd been four inches taller, she'd have been strutting Paris catwalks with Naomi Campbell. Leanne had all the equipment to cause a stir and a car crash.

One incident nailed her in a nutshell. On a very hot day, apparently, some old Glasgow cock was cruising down the road in his 'Roller', while Leanne walked the pavement wearing nearly nothing and stilettos. He must have clocked her a second too long, mounted the kerb and hit a lamp post. Since then, people have called Leanne 'Car Crash'.

But, really, she was turbocharged with clean lines. Leanne hated anything not all buttoned up and neat and tidy. Her toenails were as well maintained and manicured as her hands, which tells you a lot about her attention to personal detail, even in places not every fella was lucky enough to see.

Bit of a variety act was Leanne, but she wasn't the only pebble on my beach. I'd never been able to stick with anyone long. Leanne's dad, Alan Arneil, who I'd never met, was a famous rally driver with a shelf stuffed full of trophies to prove it. He'd heard I knew Leanne but word on the street was he wasn't much happy about it.

'There … all done,' she said, blowing the hair off my shirt and trousers on to her skin-tight blue jeans, white pumps and the white sheet she'd laid on the carpet underneath the pine chair I was sitting on. I got up and she moved the chair into the corner of the room. She folded the sheet into a neat parcel, opened the window wide, flapped the sheet into the breeze – getting rid of every last hair from my head – folded the sheet back up and placed it neatly on a table. She was ready for her next customer.

'Anything else, sir?' she asked, running her tongue lightly across her top lip in slow motion.

'Can I give you a tip?' I smiled.

About an hour later, I'd just lit a cigarette when my mobile rang. I gave a smoky hello and coughed. It was Garry McMillan. I had known Garry since boxing shorts were so big that you had to tie them up with a belt or a piece of rope. I hadn't seen him for some time, but my nose told me what this might be about. I smelt trouble in the wind. Nothing was ever straightforward with him. 'Scott, need to speak,' he said. 'Tell me when you're finished. I'll come and meet you.' Finished what? I thought.

'Okay bro, I'll get back to you when I'm home.' I had no intention of calling him back today, if ever.

I pulled in and parked my car in the garage, which was behind my apartment building, when my phone rang in my kit bag on the back seat. Someone once told me that I had

360 degrees of awareness, which on the streets, in this neck of the woods, was more important than in the ring, where at least there was a referee. But on the streets and in the ring, anyone can turn a blind eye, to an extent, if they had a wad of notes stuffed in their pocket. The motto around here was 'watch your back' or get a minder to do that for you. Where I was from, safety in numbers didn't just apply to teenage gals.

With heightened awareness, I opened the car door, got out and reached into the back for my kit bag, then I heard a car drive up and stop. With the engine still ticking over, I heard a car door open, then another. I didn't hear them close. Then I heard footsteps. I turned just as a baseball bat came down on me. There was no time to dodge or catch it. Whack!

I spun like a top, and the pain rocketed straight through me. I managed to stay on my feet for a second or two, then I hit the deck. I was barely conscious. Instinctively, I threw my hands up to protect myself from further punishment, but I was being pole-axed.

I began to slip away and could feel blood trickling down the side of my face. I smelled it in the ether, too. That rusty aroma of blood can be the onset of death. If this was only round one, it felt like I'd need the attention of an undertaker pretty soon. Two other men joined the attack. I was being punched, manhandled and bundled into the back of a blood-red Honda. I was pinned by muscle, bad intentions and steel.

An arm was locked as tight as a wound-up vice around my neck, and I could feel a knife-tip stuck into my side. If I fought back or moved an inch, the knife was going in. Once

I made out their faces, I was consumed with disbelief and shock. These guys weren't strangers. I knew them all, for fuck's sake. What's going on? Over the years, they'd worked with me and for me along the way. We'd been lads for a long time.

Sitting in the back of the car, the only defence I had up my sleeve were words – maybe rationalising a bit – so I went for it in spite of the odds. Was this about a woman? Come on! It can't be. Or, maybe it's about …?

'You cunts … what is this?!'

'Shurrup.'

'About what? A fucking tart?!'

One of them stabbed me in the leg. The five-inch, lock-back blade cut clean into my leg, just above the knee. It should've hurt like hell, but I felt nothing. My mind raced. None of this stacked up. I regarded these guys. We grew up together and I boxed with them. My grandfather was friends with their fathers.

Mother of God, was there no honour? This was Judas Iscariot in triplicate, and they were here to give me a Glasgow-style kiss. I wasn't thinking about dying yet but death had me lined up in its sights. GBH was starting to turn into RIP. I stopped thinking and started operating from a different place – pure survival instincts.

We were driving fast into deserted countryside, three or four minutes from where I lived on Hamilton's outskirts. I was nailed down in the back of the car. I knew I was going to get hammered one way or another. They were in too deep now to stop. Everyone was yelling and screaming. It was chaos inside that car.

McMillan and the two boys I can't name seemed pumped full of steroids and dope. They were deranged. I tried to say something, and the cunt in the passenger seat turned around and punched me smack on the nose. He was a boxer, so he could hit. I felt my nose crack like a stick. Now I was bleeding in three places. I wished I had a friend or two here to even the odds and settle this. I knew these fuckers would happily cut me into pieces, leaving me dead, buried and forgotten.

We got to Mutton Hall Road, where I did my roadwork every day. They pulled up to a halt in a side lane. It was too quiet, not even the birds were singing, and there was nobody around. Not a house in sight. People had been found dead in these parts.

Words weren't going to help me now. I was in a last-chance saloon. I knew I had to make a move because these guys were going to kill me here. I still didn't know why. But I couldn't die without taking a shot at living. One of them eyeballed me. An index finger beckoned me to get out. I couldn't make a move yet. The knife was still pinned hard into my side. Another of my assailants opened the car boot. I could hear tools clattering on to the ground. I was praying they didn't have a chainsaw. When he came back into view, he was clutching a baseball bat in one hand and a claw hammer in the other. And he was smiling. This wasn't going to be a beating; it was an execution.

If so, these fuckers were going about it in a very slow way. One well-directed 9mm bullet would've worked. I started being appreciative about ways it seemed I wouldn't die. At least they hadn't poured petrol all over me and slung in a Zippo.

Fuck them. Push had come to shove. If I was going to die, I was taking one of them with me. I noticed the central locking was off. I leapt out of the car, fast as a rat, slammed the door on the knife coming after me, trapping a hand in the process, which gave me a split-second before a baseball bat slammed across the front of my shins.

I grabbed the biggest of the three, stuck my fingers square into his eye and tried to gouge it out. He screamed with pain. I hoped I'd blinded the bastard. The driver pulled a ball-bearing gas gun. I heard two shots blow in quick succession. *Bam bam*. I went down like a falling tree in a hurricane. I must've gone out like a light, but now back, but only just. Then I heard a voice from deep inside me. *Play dead*. The last thing I can remember was a hammer smashing on to my ankle.

Barely conscious, I laid like a big lump of granite rock, going nowhere, and held my breath. With my eyes shut tight but ears wide open, I could hear the clunking sounds of the car doors closing: one, two, three. The engine fired up and I heard the car rumble away, but then it stopped.

Jesus, are they coming back? I asked myself from the half-distance of being neither there nor anywhere. My clock was definitely ticking. Out of the corner of one slit of an eye, I could see the car reversing slowly towards me. It stopped, then silence. I kept watching with my ears. They were probably checking to see if I was still breathing. I stayed completely still and held my breath. If they'd had even one brain cell between them, they would've run me over.

'He's dead. Let's get the fuck out of here.' The car sped away, with the sound of the engine evaporating into a distant night. As I sucked in a lungful of cool-night air, a dimmer switch turned off my lights.

Someone or something switched me back on like an alarm clock, and my eyes opened, buzzing like light bulbs. I had no idea how long I'd been here, where *here* was, or why. I didn't know anything. I was freezing cold and shivering, even though sweat was clogging my eyebrows and dripping into my eyes. I listened to the sounds of the night and heard the distant barking of a dog. Otherwise, there was nothing but graveyard silence until I heard a church bell tolling the time. I counted the chimes – 11. Jesus, I'm still alive. Or am I?

Then the pain hit me like electricity. The agony was indescribable. It was not here nor there. The pain wasn't in any one particular place, but in waves throughout me. I felt like I was on fire. Then I heard a voice, with an echo wrapped around it, from deep inside me. I'd heard the voice before but was never able to place it. *Get up.*

For a split second, the voice overwhelmed the pain. I tried to move but everything in my being felt broken. The hammer and the other weapons they'd used must've broken my arm, hand, leg and foot. I was immobile like a car with a dead battery. With a deep breath, I managed to raise my head a fraction then let it fall back on to the cold ground. At the very least, I knew I had been able to move. I wasn't dead.

Get up, the voice said again. I had to get out of there. They could come back. I was amazed they hadn't yet. The voice spoke to me again. *Sing – sing*. Sing? I couldn't remember any songs to save my life. I tried to roll over, so I could crawl or drag myself along. Then, suddenly, from nowhere, I remembered the words we sang at Sunday school when I was a kid.

'One more step along the world we go ...'

I couldn't remember the rest of the song. I kept repeating those words, over and over. Deep in my soul, the words gave me a shot of energy. Jesus was working with me. I felt it. He was in my corner. I focused on that idea and a faded childhood memory. On the wall of my Sunday school, a picture of Jesus hung in a simple wooden frame. While we sat and learned about Christ and miracles, occasional rays of mid-afternoon sunshine would shine on that picture and brighten the room.

The memory was the push-start for my dead battery. I started crawling on my hands, using my elbows to drag myself along, scraping the skin off my knees and elbows. I was throbbing like a road drill. I didn't know which part of me was in more pain. I tried to transcend it, rise above it and deal with it. But something told me the pain was keeping me awake and alive, so I began using it like a friend. I started welcoming the pain.

Extra-sensory skills, which I didn't know I had, guided me inch by inch to a pitch-black country road. I couldn't see a blind thing, but I knew the road. This was where I did my roadwork, so I knew I had a choice of sorts. Either I could crawl into a ditch and stay there until daylight, if daylight ever came, or crawl along the middle of the road.

If I used the road, I risked getting hit by a car because the driver wouldn't see me. There was a flash of lightning. I counted the seconds – one, two … then heard a roll of thunder. A quarter-moon severed the clouds, like a knife, and for a split second I could see. Left or right? Fuck it, I'm going to take a chance. I went left, crawled into the middle of the road and looked ahead. There was a pinprick of light in the distance – maybe 300 yards away, hard to say. A streetlight, a house, a stationary motorbike with its headlight on, my imagination? It didn't matter. I just needed a target to aim for – a lighthouse to navigate the ship.

It took an hour on the road from hell to get to the light, but it felt like a lifetime. I wasn't even sure that I was still really alive. Maybe my nerves were just waiting to give up the ghost. Feeling the cat's eyes with my hands kept me in the middle of the road. I kept singing and not a single vehicle drove by, not even a hearse. My imagination was spinning, too. I expected to get run over by an ice cream van, with its windows blown out by a shotgun, or pissed on by a passing dog cocking its leg. If I hadn't been match-fit, I'd have been a goner.

But something else was keeping me going. I'd connected with something, tucked away in my core that must've been waiting for this day to reveal itself. I wasn't alone. Every now and then, when I had to, I would stop and lay my head down against the damp road for a couple of minutes, gathering up a shot of resolve and energy to carry on. I could've talked myself out of this and just lay there, closed my eyes and died like an injured animal after it drags itself into the undergrowth. Instead, I sang at the top of my voice, though I'd never been able to sing. 'One more step along the world …'

Round 2

Banged Up

19 May 2004

I couldn't translate the whispering into words. My eyelids didn't want to open, so I gave them a very gentle nudge. Through slit eyes, I saw mist. There were no boundaries or corners, just a hinterland between here and there, like a whiteout in wonderland. I thought a white rabbit, with a pocket watch, would come tearing along in a minute saying, 'I'm late.'

I began to make out vague shapes, no more than flimsy, ghostly silhouettes. It was like coming around from being knocked out. When you don't know if you're here, there or anywhere. It's a blur. Then you hear noise and a ceiling of faces gradually comes into view. 'Was I knocked out? Was he better?'

'Scott.' It sounded like my mother's voice. 'Scott.'

I focused on the direction the voice came from. I could see just a little more clearly through a curtain of eyelashes. Mum looked worn out; she'd had a rough time of things and now this had come on top of everything else.

'Scott? Scott, speak to me.' Her voice was closer now. Her words were filled with anxiety washed out with tears. I could see my mother, who looked thinner than usual and lined with worry, weary eyes that hadn't slept. Around Mum were two gals I'd been messing around with and my current girlfriend, Fiona. It looked like I was in for a verbal mugging of the hen variety.

Not one of the gals knew I was seeing the other two, but by now, the cat must've be out of the bag.

Before anyone could say another word, a nurse, who was a dead ringer for Lulu aged 20, came to my rescue. 'If you feel pain, press this to self-administer morphine. We can't have you being distressed.' She put a PCA [patient-controlled analgesia] pump in my right hand. I pressed it slowly, whistling up a blast of morphine. I pressed it once more for good measure. Then a third time for luck. It denied me any more. If anyone invents a pump without a limiter, they'd make a fortune. I felt a stream of cool liquid flood my veins and the whiteness moved back in; a rolling mist on Hamilton Moors just before dark. I remember being almost lost in that mist.

When I woke up, Nurse 'Rescue' was holding my wrist and looking at her watch. She was surrounded by a halo of light. I looked left, right and beyond. She appeared to be the only woman in my room. Thank God.

'Am I alive, Angel?' I whispered.

'Yes, you are, by some miracle. How are you feeling today?' I felt like death warmed up. She was a nurse, so I could say what I felt like. If anyone else had asked me, I'd have said 'fine'.

'Like shit, sick and groggy. Like I've been slugged and drugged.'

'Do you want a sip of water?' she asked. She even had Lulu's smile. I remember thinking, 'I must ask her to sing for me one day.'

Over cracked lips set around a bone-dry mouth, I creaked out a 'yes'. She held a little plastic bottle with a sucker on it, like wee babies drink, and gave me one suck. Then she took it away. 'Your lips look like they need some Vaseline. You had six visitors yesterday; must be pretty popular,' she smiled.

This angel must have to cope with all kinds of lunatics in this place. Maybe she's trained to be sweet like this to everybody, or maybe the hospital gives its nurses Valium to ease their days. Whatever the reason, I counted myself lucky. I could've had some smelly old boot of a woman tending me. I stared into her sparkling blue eyes.

'Six? I remember seeing four.'

'Two policemen. And a lot of people have called, asking how you are, but we can't speak to them unless they're relatives.'

'How can you tell who's who?'

'Actually, we can't.' Probably those fuckers who tried to kill me, I thought.

'And a woman was here with you all night after your operation. She was very distressed. We talked for hours.'

'Oh yeah, who?'

'Leanne. You must mean a lot to her.'

'Leanne was here?'

'She never left your side. We talked most of the night. She said you had saved her life when she was having a hard time. Leanne feels it was a miracle that her parents helped save yours.'

'Maybe,' I muttered.

I knew Leanne's parents *had* saved my life, of course, but I didn't want to think of the two instances as tit for tat. As it turned out, that tiny bit of light – the beacon that shone off the road from hell – was the home of Leanne's parents. They took me in and got me here. Even still, I had helped Leanne before because I cared. Neither she nor her parents owed me anything, especially my life.

'There's no maybe about it from what she told me. Anyway, Scott, the doctor will be along in a minute to explain an operation you're going to need. Press that button if you need me. Your wish is my command.'

'When I'm back on my feet, say that again,' I smiled. 'Oh, hang on, actually there is.'

'Yes?'

'Is there anything to read here?'

'Such as?'

'A Bible.'

'Funny,' she said and skipped out of the room.

This would've been paradise if I hadn't been so banged up. I love women in nurse's uniforms almost as much as I hate women in police uniforms, unless it's a stripagram and still I'm wary. Nurses are trained to know what makes a guy tick but even with all the nurses about, I just wanted to see Leanne. However, less romantic thoughts stayed at the forefront of my mind.

If those three fuckers paid me a visit, I was a sitting duck in this bed. I would've asked my pals if they could smuggle a gun but the cop outside my door frisked everyone, and nobody got in without a pass. All I had was a bedpan and I wasn't sure I had the strength to hurl anything.

What I could spout about the attack that they didn't want anybody to know. Even if the police were outside the door, they'd be no fucking use against men carrying more than a fistful of lilies and a handful of grapes. Before I could measure my reach to the bedpan, I heard a key turn in the door. Two men in white coats entered the room towing a middle-aged staff sister. She locked the door behind the doctors.

'I'm Doctor Wilson. How are you, Mr Dixon?' He looked like he was the top dog. An Englishman who'd crossed the border to find out what life's really like, he seemed like a rugby type. The other guy, who looked like a kid doctor, must've been a trainee. The staff sister had a face and persona as starched as her uniform, but I could tell she was putting it on. Her job was to impress the pants off Doctor Wilson – on the ward and in bed after the Christmas party. It was written all over her erect nipples. Really, she wasn't bad looking, if you fancied older birds.

'Call me Scott. Mr Dixon is my grandfather.'

'Well, Scott, considering your ordeal, as well as everything we had to do, you look remarkably well. In 20 years, I've rarely seen so many injuries on one human being who lived. You must have a guardian angel.' The doc picked up my hospital notes that hung from the bottom of my bed, glanced at them, shook his head and put them back. He wasn't mucking around.

'There's a whole catalogue of damage, Scott. Knife wounds and you were shot twice. We removed two ball bearings the size of marbles, presumably fired from a gas-powered gun. Your skull is fractured. We've had to pin bones and insert a steel plate into your arm. You've got severe tendon damage. Your ankle bone has a hole in it, which is a new challenge for the surgeons. They've never seen that before. You have a lot of broken bones and fractures. You've had a blood transfusion and …' His voice faded.

'And what?'

'Well, you had a seizure during the six-hour operation, and your heart stopped. Not long enough to cause any permanent damage, as far as we know, but we are monitoring that. You are in high-dependency, so you'll be under constant observation, and the Hamilton police have insisted you remain under lock and key for your own safety. Only the police, allocated staff members, close family and anyone cleared by the police have access to this room.' He cleared his throat. 'Oh yes, one last thing. Have you heard of dropped foot?'

'Not until now. Is that like hobbled, a tendon thing?'

'Similar, so let's hope that's not the case. Otherwise, you may not be able to lift your foot from the ankle again.'

This must be a trial for the hospital. The staff were regularly attacked here by people they were trying to help. I'd heard stories. It was bedlam on Friday and Saturday nights.

They should've got danger money or bodyguards. They had enough shit and violence to deal with as it was. I couldn't help but think about my assailants coming, once they found out I had survived.

'If the people who did this decide to come here to finish it, not even a steel door can stand in their way. Your doors are plywood,' I said.

'There's a policeman outside right now.'

'Same difference.'

'They've asked me to give them the all-clear to interview you.'

'Not today,' I replied.

'Out of professional curiosity, how did you survive this?' he asked. Usually, I wouldn't have said anything, but I answered. It must've been the dope.

'I heard a voice.' He looked at me over his half-moon glasses.

'What did the voice say?'

'Sing.' He shot me a look and scratched his head. He must've thought I was either kidding or nuts.

'By rights, you should be dead. But I read about an SAS soldier who battled on with six bullets in him, so I'm open-minded. Maybe it's adrenalin.'

'How long will I be in here?' His face told me he didn't know.

'Let's take it a week at a time. Meanwhile, I need to get your temperature down.'

I could see he was thinking months, wheelchairs, crutches, a walking stick and a lifetime of physio. I knew it. And what the fuck was dropped foot? I was living but would I fight again? And if I couldn't fight, would I still be living? What a mess.

They left, and I heard the door lock. I was wondering why my grandfather hadn't been to see me yet. There had to be a good reason. I don't co-operate with the Old Bill, so they'd get nothing out of me. I pressed the morphine pump. As the drug's warmth began to course through my veins, I started thinking about Hamilton and Papa.

With none of the guiding lights that I was fortunate to have, kids had fuck-all else to do in Hamilton. With no prospects or motivation, there was no point in attending school, because there was little chance of meaningful work afterwards. Really, all available options were risky: an education, football, boxing, crime, an undertaker or a miracle. Those were the only five ways out of this hellhole.

I was one of the luckier few, though. I was loved, cared for, watched over and guided constantly by three people. Along with a caring mum, my grandmother was the sweetest creature in the world. Gran knitted jumpers, darned socks with spuds in them and conjured up tasty meals out of thin air. Scottish people aren't as tight with money as people think, but out of necessity, they watched every penny like their lives depended on it. In many cases, it did.

But outside the safety of the home, it was my grandfather who kept me safe in the streets. He was a full-time, unpaid minder who watched my back; a mentor who stepped into my father's shoes when he walked out; a perfect grandad-come-dad double-act who I called Papa. Over the years, he worked as a security officer, taxi driver, lorry driver and long-distance coach driver. He did whatever it took to put bread on the table. Both my guiding light and the rudder in the storm guiding me towards that light, Papa not only understood the difference between right and wrong; he practised it every waking day.

When I was young, I'd lie awake with my boxing gloves on and listen for him to come back home. He'd walk in, see me in the hallway in the half-light, laugh, then drop to his knees. We'd spend an hour dodging and weaving and throwing punches. He blocked them all, except one night when I banged him on the nose. Maybe he had let me get one shot in. I'll never know.

'Sorry.'

'You're getting the hang of this, son,' he said, smiling while rubbing his nose with his thumb. 'Time for bed. Don't forget to say your prayers.'

One day, he got me a pet rabbit I named Snowy because it was white. He also built me a treehouse when we got a house. Up in the treehouse, I saw the world from another point of view. There was a photo of me aged two up in the treehouse. Wearing boxing gloves and headgear, which were actually earphones, I had my arms tucked up tight against my body, and my face wore a defiant, fixed stare. It was my treehouse after all.

My grandfather taught me how to box. He showed me the ropes as soon as I could walk. He was always in my corner, teaching me the tricks of the trade, and he knew those tricks better than most. We'd spend hours in the gym together, with him on the pads. 'Higher, harder, middle, lower, step back, lead with your left,' he'd shout. 'Think of your left not as a fist, but a barn door to shut opponents out.'

He only let me rest when I was completely out of breath. 'In the shower now,' he'd say. 'Five minutes, hot as you can stand it, then five minutes cold. And hurry up. Gran will have supper ready.' While other kids were boozing, buzzing on gas, puffing grass and chasing girls, I was at the gym, training and sparring because he told me to. Resistance was useless. 'You can thank me for this later,' he'd say.

Papa trained and mentored a lot of champs. Eventually, he became the president of the Scottish Boxing Hall of Fame. Toby Dixon wasn't feared, which is easy to accomplish, he was respected. People came to him for advice and guidance when they were afraid, broke or broken. He sorted people out, usually with an invisible touch. People rarely knew he'd engineered a solution. He didn't want any thanks. There were many trainers, but few teachers like him. Today, people call him 'the Scientist of Boxing', and he was. He studied the art more than anyone else, then applied his knowledge to the game while maxing a fighter's potential by getting to know them personally.

'What goes on outside the ring, in the real world, is every bit as important as what goes into training and boxing. A man's mental and spiritual health make the difference,' he would say. 'I train the whole person.' Papa was holistic long before the term was fashionable. He was also a very strict disciplinarian.

One day, I met him at the gym at 5pm to start training at 5pm.

'What time do you call this, Scott?' he asked sharply.

'Five, like you said.'

'Then you're a half-hour late. At 4.30, you get changed and loosened up, then we start work at five.' He also had an expression: 'Third time unlucky.' It meant that if someone, no matter who they were, was late three times – finito!

Throughout my life, I wanted to be just like him. He was a very wise man. There were 13 words he had said that always stuck with me. 'A real man goes home after a hard day's work to his family.'

Growing up, I was fortunate to have two homes. I could stay with mum or with my grandparents, and both doors were always open. Living with my mother meant spending more time alone, which she found hard. She worked as a secretary for Strathclyde City Council, but the money she earned was always shy of what she needed. So, she often worked in the evening as a taxi driver. But, when I stayed with my grandparents, there was always someone there. That's not to blame my mum a jot for anything. She was and always will be, in my eyes, my mum, who always cared for me and loved me. It was just fortunate that she had the back-up of her mum and dad right on the doorstep.

From what I'd heard, it may have been a blessing that my dad walked out and never came back. He was less than a shadow on the wall in my mum's eyes and not even a memory for me. I was too young to remember anything about him. Bit by bit, Papa become my father. In my eyes, my dad did me a favour by leaving me in better hands than his own.

Over the years, my dad popped in and out of my life, every now and then, when it suited him. He would come like a fly on the wall for a quick look-see, only to fly off again. Maybe it was guilt that kept him in touch at all. He never gave Mum a penny to support us, which was why she flogged herself to death working two jobs.

Although it's easy to be mad, I probably had a lot of my dad in me. I was a bit of a drifter, always moving on. I don't know if it was the case with him, but for the most part, I blamed women. I shouldn't have, but I did. When I was a kid, I thought women were going to be like Gran: loyal, present, watching, cooking and guiding me in a motherly way. My future loves would handmake bedroom curtains from remnants they'd found in the market, place them on my windows and shroud me from the world. Life could be a disappointment when expectations and standards didn't meet, so it was easy to drift away from it sometimes.

Gran and Papa had a wonderful, steady and caring relationship. They both came from a little town called Larkhall, met at a dance hall and became sweethearts in the 1930s. That's when Gran first tasted a peach melba knickerbocker glory. She always talked about the first one and very occasionally made her own. 'I had never tasted anything so delicious in my life. I had my first one on the night your Papa proposed to me,' she'd say.

They married in the 1940s. In the 50s, they emigrated to Canada and enjoyed ten good years in Toronto. Papa even won a district amateur boxing championship in Canada. But they decided to return to Scotland because they wanted to raise a family. Both very patriotic, they wanted their children to be raised Scottish. They had two daughters, but Papa had always wanted a son, as men usually do. I think that's why he doted on me and treated me like a son.

As a long-distance lorry and coach driver, Papa was often away for weeks at a time. When Gran had me all to herself, it was okay just to be a kid. I didn't have to pretend that I was a man when I wasn't yet. My fondest memories of Gran had a lot to do with food. You couldn't walk into her house without being greeted by the smells of a homemade soup or meat pie, a gooseberry pie, a custard, or on very rare occasions, a mouth-watering peach melba knickerbocker glory in a tall glass.

As I got older, my Gran's home became an open house at all hours for friends, neighbours or young boxers from the club. Nobody ever went hungry, even when it was just a piece of toast smothered in Marmite. If she spotted a hole in my jumper or tears in the other boxers' clothes, we'd have to take them off and she'd darn it there and then.

One day, Jimmy Burns had his hands in his pockets, which used to upset Papa to no end. 'People who have their hands in their pockets are lazy and thoughtless with no ambition,' he would say. Knowing Papa was away working, Jimmy had his hands in his pockets as usual. 'Right, that's it, Jimmy. Take your trousers off now and give them to me,' Gran insisted.

'What?'

I started laughing. Gran threw me eye-daggers to make me stop.

'Take them off,' she snapped while reaching for her sewing box.

'Is there a hole in them?' he asked timidly.

'Two as it happens. Do as I say.'

Looking like his world had collapsed, Jimmy slowly kicked off his shoes, dropped his trousers, stepped out of them and handed them to Gran. He stood there in his shirt, socks and pants. Blushed to his roots, his face matched his wispy red hair. I had to pinch myself to keep from bursting out laughing again. Gran stitched up the pockets and handed the trousers back to Jimmy. Most kids love their grans, but everybody adored mine, even when she embarrassed them.

Gran also got me interested in what was lovely to the eye. Or, at least, she may have encouraged it. One day, she was trying to decide which material to use for a cotton dress from three swatches. 'Which of these do you think would suit me the best?'

'That one,' I said, pointing to the one with flowers on it. The pattern and colour were a dead match for her pale blue eyes. 'Hold it up to your cheek and let's see.' Gran did what I asked, laughing.

'Perfect,' I said.

'You're a funny one, Scott. You have an eye for beauty. One day, the gals will have to watch out,' she laughed.

Papa and Gran's devotion to religion permeated their lives and mine, reflected by the silver crosses we all wore around our necks. Gran first took me to Sunday school when I was seven. It was definitely part of their collective plan to help keep me on the straight and narrow and out of bother. Wearing a frock adorned with a tiny embroidered flower, her best shoes, a coat and a hat, she would drop me off at Sunday school. As a child, I found the stories in the Bible not only interesting, but absolutely fascinating. Moses with the Ten Commandments, God sacrificing his only son to save mankind, walking on water, the feeding of the 5,000 and the resurrection of Jesus all added a sense of wonder and reverence to my childhood.

I even found myself able to recite short passages from the Bible. That amused kids in the neighbourhood but on one occasion, when another kid pulled Wendy McBride's pigtails and hurt her, instead of punching him, I remember saying, 'Do unto others as you would have them do unto you.' He laughed and looked at me a little bewildered. Wendy gave me a lovely smile, then a lovelier kiss a few years later. I attended Sunday school regularly until I was 14. By then, I was hooked. Religion was inside me. A lot of people thought my obsession was a bit extreme. Others use to make fun of me, but I didn't do anything by halves. I believed and always would, and that's all there was to it. All or nothing.

While Sunday school and Gran's house were sanctuaries, the neighbourhood's shadows always crept right outside their doors. Neighbourhood kids always stole stuff from the shops, mostly sweets but really anything that fitted in their pocket. One day, I stole three Mars bars from the local shop and Papa found them while fixing my bedroom light. He descended the aluminium stepladder smattered with dried paint and handed me a £1 note. 'Take them back and pay for them. Bring me the change,' he said.

Fearing a thrashing, I knew I had let him down and tarnished the family name. I was now Scott Dixon, a common thief.

'What do I say?' I asked, sheepish and embarrassed.

'Say to Mrs Campbell, "I stole three Mars bars. I'm sorry and won't do it again. If I pay for them, they're mine, yes?"'

'She'll go mad at me. What if she calls the police? Will you come with me?'

His typically stoic face said 'no'. It was usually hard to tell what Papa was feeling because he rarely gave anything away. And when he did speak, he only used a few meaningful words, never leaving any doubt about what those words meant. I was on my own with this.

I stood outside the corner shop for all of five minutes, waiting for it to empty. When the last person came out and closed the door, I walked in. The old-fashioned doorbell made its tinny metallic sound a few times, announcing my arrival.

'Hello Scott,' said Mrs Campbell with a smile. 'What can I do for you today?'

'I have come to say I'm sorry.'

'For what?' she asked, furling her forehead into a few more lines than usual.

'For stealing these,' I said, holding out the three Mars bars.

'You know stealing is against the law?'

'Yes.'

'You know it's one of the Ten Commandments? You go to Sunday school. What is it, tell me?'

'Thou shalt not steal.' I wanted the shop floor to crack open and swallow me up. 'I'm sorry, Mrs Campbell. I won't do it again.'

'Well, make sure of that. At least you had the strength and courage to say you're sorry. I imagine your grandfather sent you.'

I didn't answer. I handed her a £1 note and she handed me the change. I left with the Mars bars as quickly as I could. On the way back from the shop, with Papa's change safely out of view and three Mars bars in my pocket, I ran into bullyboy Scott McCann. He lived one floor under us in the flats.

'Hiya, Scott. Empty your pockets.'

'Piss off.' He hit me three times before I could get one in: on my nose, smack in the eye and on my forehead. Then he walked away. As I watched him, I felt inside my pockets to make sure Papa's change was still there, turned around and ran for my building crying. There was no lift, so the journey from ground level to our flat was about 100 concrete steps, but it's 1,000 when you feel like I was feeling. Out of breath and still crying, I got to our flat. Blood was streaming out of my nose, and a bruise was swelling up my eye. Papa was standing in the doorway, looking down at me. If he was concerned, he wasn't letting on.

'Why are you crying?'

'Scott McCann punched me.'

Papa took a mint out of his trouser pocket and crushed it between his teeth. He put his hand on my shoulder. 'Go down, find him and sort it out, then come back and I'll let you in.'

The door closed on me. I walked down the staircase very slowly, considering every downward step I took into a complete unknown. I had to challenge not only Scott McCann, but myself. Scott was outside bothering another lad. I took a deep breath. 'Hey, come here,' I shouted.

As he was walking over to me, looking menacing, I quickly glanced upwards. Papa was leaning out of the window with his elbows resting on the sill, his face cupped in his hands. He was not letting me back into the flat until I bashed this guy up. I was a bit scared. McCann was older than me and heavier. I remembered what Papa had told me. 'Nice straight jabs, then left and right combinations.' I also remembered what he said about speed. 'Count the beat with my name: pa-pa, pa-pa, pa-pa.'

Before he could make a fist, I hit Scott twice in the face. A straight left to his nose, then a straight right bang on his chin. He was on his arse, looking dazed and crying. When

I got back upstairs, the door was wide open. I was greeted with the smell of bacon frying on the gas ring and Al Jolson singing in my ears.

After tea, we watched Ali knock out Liston on the video. It was a lesson in super skill. Hit fast, shoot straight, don't get caught, travel the distance and bide your time. Liston kept coming at him like a freight train, so there's only one way to deal with that – speed. Float like a butterfly, sting like a bee. 'Scott, have you done your homework?' Gran asked, interrupting us. It was fine, I liked school and looked forward to it. All the subjects appealed to me, even art.

Papa was always gentle and considerate with Gran, listening to her problems, chatting about this and that. Occasionally, they'd hold hands for no particular reason, just silent communication I suppose. One day, I'd just got home from the gym and when I opened the door, I heard a tune I'd never heard before. Later, I discovered it was 'Misty', sung by Johnny Mathis, 'misty the moment you get near ...' Papa and Gran swayed slowly together, cheek to cheek, singing the words in tune to one another. I snuck away to my room and closed the door. Even though it was my grandma's birthday, I learned what 'three's a crowd' meant that day.

When I was young, I was mad for football and a promising striker. That's the key position on the field, where the action and glory is, but boxing was in my genes and blood. The two sports were a close-run thing. I was never without a football in my hands or near my feet. Papa painted a goal on the brick wall near where he parked his car, and he'd watch me shooting for the corners. 'You need a goalie,' he said, walking over to the wall. He moved from side to side, but I got the ball past him most of the time. 'You might want to try out for the Glasgow Rangers when you're older,' he said. 'You've got good movement and can kick hard. There's a lot more money in football than boxing, if you make it big.'

Even at that age, I knew that I couldn't give 100 per cent to boxing and 100 per cent to football. I didn't have 200 per cent to give, but I tried. I played football whenever I could and did get a shot at the big time when I was in my mid-teens, albeit by chance.

When I was 12, I went to Hamilton Grammar School. The move up to a much bigger school made me apprehensive. Generally, I kept quiet and to myself. The massive, imposing, sand-coloured brick building was formerly Hamilton Academy, which gave its name to Hamilton Academical, the football club, which was founded in 1874 by the rector and pupils. Football was in its history and throughout its corridors, which were full of framed photographs and paintings.

The game was the school's passion, whereas boxing was considered a bit of a taboo. The headmaster, who was nicknamed Jimmy Eyebrows because of his huge Groucho Marx eyebrows, thought it should be banned, and he wasn't shy of saying so. The only time I ever got into bother with the headmaster was after fighting some Catholic lads at their school. But my physical education and football teacher, Mr Walker, had a soft spot for me. He liked my dedication to sports and picked me for the school's football team. When I was 14, he also picked me for the school's counties team.

At that time, my mum's sister, Auntie Jennifer, started seeing the Rangers' Davie Cooper after meeting him at the Sands Club. Davie, always my hero, was reckoned to be the best left-winger in Scotland. I could hardly believe my luck. Knowing Davie made me a bit of a school celebrity. The girls wanted to know me, just in case they got the chance to meet Davie, who was a real pin-up boy and every bit as good-looking as George Best in his great Manchester United days. My mates were always asking questions about him and trying to get tickets from me.

Davie use to get me into Ibrox, the Rangers stadium. On matchdays, I'd be sitting with Papa in the dugout, where the players had their complimentary seats. Davie took us to the trophy room, the home changing room, and he even let us walk through the tunnel, which few people got to do when there was a match on. He gave me a Rangers shirt signed by all the players and a club tie with the emblem on it, which I still have to this day. I met Graeme Souness, Ally McCoist, Ian Durrant, Mark Walters, Terry Hurlock, Robert Fleck, Paul Gascoigne and Terry Butcher.

One day, Davie suggested I try out with the Rangers, and he must've opened a few doors to make that happen. Nobody could believe it, especially me. I had two trials but was told I didn't have the skills, which was a blow at the time. I hardly ever kicked a football with the same intensity after that, but always stayed an avid Rangers fan.

After the trials, I went totally into boxing much to Papa's delight. But, if I had made it with the Glasgow Rangers, I knew Papa would've been cock-a-hoop about that, too. I left Hamilton Grammar with GCSEs in science, maths, English, history, art, religious instruction and PE, as well as a few general sports and football trophies. I got a good education and felt I had made the most out of school.

While I got a whiff of football success, boxing never left my blood. When I was seven, I started going to the Hamilton ABC gym, located six bus stops away on a rough housing estate. For the most part, reprobates went there to train. That's where I first met the three people who tried to kill me. They were all a few years younger than me.

I was lanky and light, and at the time there was nobody to fight in my weight class. Mark Young was the only contender my age, but he was three sacks of potatoes heavier than me. The 'incredible bulk' was so tubby that Papa had to get him a pair of men's boxing shorts. He could swing but I could dodge and weave and jab – pa-pa. In those days, there were no headguards like today. If you got slugged, you got slugged.

A bigger challenge happened a few years later. I was 11 and fighting gypsy-boy Joe Gillan from Motherwell, our town's arch enemy. Scotland was very territorial. Even with superior skills, I couldn't get near the guy because of his reach. I went toe to toe, which was not my style unless I was pushed.

After the fight, Papa took me to the side. 'Nothing is beyond your reach, son. You're a natural at this.' Sometimes, a few well-chosen words spoken at the right moment was all the encouragement you needed. After a few years passed, I turned pro and became hell-bent on success. In those days, I didn't know what fear, failure or fear of failure meant.

In the hospital, in between consciousness, I felt a hand on mine. I'd felt it many times before. I opened my eyes and saw Papa with his mass of mad-white hair just like Mum's, only hers was blonde with ringlets like Goldilocks. The second I saw him, tears started streaming from my eyes.

'It's okay, son, slow down. Take a breath.' I checked out the room. Nobody else was there so far as I could see. I was choked to silence. He was there beside me at last, but I couldn't stem the flood.

'I'm sorry, Papa, it's the fucking morphine. I'm not myself,' I said, choking on the words.

'No need to swear, Scott. Who did this to you? I reckon I know, but I need to hear you say the three names that come to my mind.' He looked at me wanting to hear the truth.

'Not sure.'

'Tell me,' he said quietly.

I knew he probably already knew. It was in his eyes. But if I pushed it, he'd make calls and I didn't want to lose him – or risk it. He was my rock and meant everything to me. He spoke in a soft, fatherly way, a way I'd not heard many times before. 'Tell me. You're all we've got, son.' I couldn't stop the tears. All of my regrets started coming out of my eyes.

'Okay, Scott. I've got a card for you – and this,' he said, pressing something metal in my hand. He closed my fingers over it, ran his open hand over my forehead, got up, unlocked the door and left without looking back. I heard the door lock on the other side. My hand stayed clenched for an hour. When I slowly opened it, my hands were chalk white and devoid of feeling. On my palm was a silver cross and a chain that felt warm. I slipped it over my head.

I opened the envelope, removed a 'get well' card and looked inside. There were messages of hope and encouragement, signed by Terry Spinks, Henry Cooper, Frank Bruno, Nigel Benn, Dick McTaggart, Billy Walker, Freddie Mack, Ray Caulfield, Mark Rowe, Charlie Magri, Alan Rudkin, Larry Paul, Reg Gutteridge, Mickey Duff, Mary Powell, Mickey O'Sullivan, Steve Powell, Billy Aird and Jimmy Batten. Why did these guys give a fuck? I appreciated the card but didn't feel like I deserved it.

Papa, who was close to a lot of current and ex-boxers, had done this for me. He must've done a postal 'round robin', sending the card all over the place to get the signatures. Or, maybe he had taken it from place to place, person to person to get it done for me. Why wasn't I more like him? One last tear fell from my chin and landed on the card. I dried the card on my bed sheet, which smudged one of the names. This wasn't only a message, this was a sign. It was time. *Get up*, Scott.

My manager at the time, Alex Morrison, got a pass from the police and came to see me. I could see how upset he was. He didn't say much but must've spoken to the *Daily Record*. The next day, the paper wrote:

Battered boxer Scott Dixon will fight again, a leading promoter said yesterday. Alex Morrison saw the former Commonwealth welterweight champ in hospital last night and said later the whole sport felt 'total revulsion' over the savage assault. He said there is still a possibility that Scott, who was left for dead, can box at the top level again.

Glasgow-based Morrison was still in shock over the abduction and deliberate maiming of Scott, 27. Morrison said: 'There's no doubt he suffered brutal injuries. For most people, breaks like that could leave them crippled. But Scott is young and very fit and I think he can come back from this and resume his career. Mentally, he seems very positive.'

Yesterday, *The Record* exclusively revealed how Scott was threatened with a sword and kidnapped just yards from his home in Hamilton and taken to an isolated country road. There, he was stabbed five times in the leg, battered with a baseball bat and a hammer and shot. He was held down while his legs were each broken in two places. Scott crawled for almost an hour on the road before raising the alarm. A police spokesman said last night: 'We are following a positive line of inquiry.'

After the article, Mum and Papa came to see me because *News of the World* reporter Nigel Weston was coming for an interview. They wanted to make sure it wasn't a hoax or something more sinister. Weston had called Mum and said he'd got the all-clear from the police to visit. But, for some reason, my mum hadn't liked the sound of his voice. She could be very canny about things. 'He was very persistent and kept calling. It was all a bit too pushy for my liking,' she said. 'Maybe just my imagination, but I don't like you being stuck in here.'

They were paying me for the story, which I wasn't going to tell in full. They didn't know that, but I hadn't earned a penny since I'd been in the hospital. When the reporter came, it was one of the hottest June days we had ever had. Weather here was normally dismal. Today, it was 32°C outside and more like 40°C inside with the radiators on. There was no way of turning them off without using a crowbar.

There was a knock on the door and a nurse I hadn't seen before walked in with a massive guy in a black suit, white shirt, tie and sunglasses. He was sweating like a pig. I shot Papa a glance. The guy reached into his inside pocket. Papa leapt up to chin him, while my mum threw herself on me. In the nick of time, he pulled out a black dictaphone from his jacket pocket. Looking rattled, the guy quickly said, 'I'm Nigel Weston. God, it's hot in here. Have I come at a bad time?'

That's how wired we were. We couldn't trust a soul, save for close family members and friends. I gave the interview, avoiding any specifics about the attack. I told him I couldn't remember anything – obviously memory loss. He looked unconvinced but didn't push it. He did want to know about my future in boxing, though. I was pretty vague about boxing as well, but I was being truthfully vague about that. I had no idea what shape I was in, would be in or what prospects I had, if any. I could be permanently crippled. He took some photos of me in bed with my mum sitting next to me and Papa standing next to her. He offered me £500, which I accepted, then he left.

'Mum, when the money arrives, I want you to have it.'

'No.'

'Yes. Put it towards a holiday. You've always wanted to go to Malta. Go and stay with your friend Alison.' Her best gal-pal Alison had gone to Malta, leaving behind a very bad situation in Hamilton, and she'd never looked back. Now, she was hooked up and happy with a guy who owned two restaurants. Alison managed one of them. I thought that something good might turn up and happen like that for my mum. She deserved to be happy, instead of fretting and struggling to survive all the time.

'We'll see, Scott,' she said. 'You just get some rest.'

After a few minutes, everyone said their goodbyes and left. I quickly drifted off. I was fighting Sonny Liston in New York, and the announcers hailed it as the greatest mismatch in boxing history. Everything and everyone in his corner looked larger than life, especially him. He looked like a man mountain. The bell rang. He marched towards me like a man always on his front foot. His eyes blazed as he rotated his gloves. I needed to stay out of his way for as long as possible. I whizzed around the ring like a fly, then leapt through the ropes and ran towards the tunnel.

When I woke up, I was dripping in sweat with a hollow, sunken feeling. I didn't know if I could ever box again. My mind starting racing. Did I even want to be a boxer? Was this what Papa wanted for me, or did I just want to prove myself to him? I was overcome with feelings of doubt and dread. I'd climbed a few mountains, but I had never felt like this. The more I thought, the more I spiralled into the bottomless depths of depression. I blinked while real tears leaked from my eyes. I could tell they were mine and not from the morphine.

In my experience, hospital routines suited the hospital not the patient, unless they were dying. At 6am on the dot, the blinds zipped up fast, then cleaners came in with buckets, mops and vacuums. The place always reeked of ammonia. Each morning, I got an excuse for a breakfast before I had time to shit. During the blur of the daily routine, I found out that the would-be assassins had been arrested. Not because of anything I'd said, which was nothing. Basically, I had only said that the attack had probably ended my boxing career. Other than that, my lips were sealed with Araldite, but someone had squealed.

I had suspected that a boxing outfit I'd refused to sign with might've been behind the attack, but there was no proof. I couldn't be sure about that – just a gut instinct that stuck. I also figured there had been more to it. The ringleader, McMillan, carried a pathetic and immature jealousy-fuelled grudge against me because I'd dated one of his ex-girlfriends.

I figured McMillan had just gone beyond what he'd been asked to do, which I assumed would've been a duffing-up at the most. As long as I live, I'll never be able to figure that out. The way and intensity in which they attacked me didn't stack up. What's almost unbelievable, but true it seemed, was that McMillan told his ex about the attack after it happened. Probably just 'pillow talk', but she then told her dad, the chief inspector. She agreed to sign a statement and go to court.

McMillan then admitted to the assault but somehow his accomplices got off. I can't say what happened at the trial because I wasn't there. But I did read the 2004 *BBC News* article.

Man jailed after hammer attack

A jealous man used a hammer to break the legs of a former Commonwealth boxer who slept with his ex-girlfriend, a jury has heard. Garry McMillan, 23, from Bellshill, was jailed at Glasgow High Court for five years for the attack. He admitted abducting Scott Dixon, 27, from his home in Hamilton and seriously assaulting him.

The judge told McMillan, himself a former schoolboy boxing champion, it was a cowardly attack. The two friends had worked and boxed together but when he heard Dixon had slept with his former girlfriend, McMillan and others took him to a remote area in Hamilton, the court heard. They dragged him from the car and hit him on his head and legs with a range of weapons, including a hammer.

His counsel denied a statement by Mr Dixon that the attack had brought his boxing career to an end. Judge Ian Peebles, who described the attack as vicious and sustained, told McMillan: 'You caused horrible injuries to this man and thereafter left him in an isolated area and he had to crawl 300 yards to get help. The whole circumstances can only be regarded as shocking.'

I moved to a twin room in my 'prison', where inmates wear pyjamas or white tie-up smocks with their arses hanging out. My hospital cellmate was named Tam. He was a laugh and I was glad of some company. I always asked him to let me borrow his crutches, but he'd be worried about causing bother with the doctors. Tam never had any visitors, probably a loner. In a funny kind of way, I liked him. We were stuck in there together and could have a good grumble. A fella of few words, he wasn't much company but was *some* company. Every time a woman came to see me, he'd peer at them through his bifocal lenses, which were thicker than the bottom of an old-fashioned soda bottle, then ask me the same question after they'd gone.

'Who was that?'

'My sister.'

'You seem very close.'

Leanne came to visit me and, for once, there was nobody else around, not even Tam. He'd been pushed off somewhere in a wheelchair.

'How are you?' Leanne asked.

'Okay.'

She held my hand. 'How are you really?'

'So so.'

'And Eleanor?'

'Mum's okay. I think, I hope.'

'She thinks you're her little prince. When you went into the operating theatre, she was beside herself. She paced the floor, sat down, stood up and sat down again. She's only a little slip of a thing. It was tragic. And your Papa looked like his world had collapsed. He was just ashen and speechless.'

I said nothing as Leanne went to the door and closed it. 'I've got some news that might cheer you up a bit,' she smiled. 'I've pulled off a bit of a flanker for you.'

'Oh yeah?'

'I've got a friend in the sports insurance business. He's set up a backdated policy in your name.'

'How did you do that?'

'Don't ask. You could get as much as a grand for being stuck in here. It's not much but it's something. It might pay you to string it out for a bit.'

'I don't have to string it out, I'm strung out. Look at me, but that's fantastic. I'll give you a cut.'

'You won't.'

The door opened, and Tam was wheeled back into the room and helped back into bed. Leanne kissed me on the lips and left.

'You've got more women than that Casanova fella. How you do it defeats the hell out of me. You must have summat I can't see,' said Tam, peering over his bifocals with the barest flicker of a smile.

I'd been off the morphine for three days and was as lethal as a cut snake. I was up and down like Tower Bridge on speed. The nurses understood how I was and why, but my mum didn't, and I'd hurt her. Yesterday, I told her never to come and see me again. I think they explained the after-effects of morphine withdrawal when she was leaving. I bloody well hoped so. I was bored rigid, bed-ridden and fidgety with a fragmented mind that pondered a fragmented future. Frankly, I was a wee bit frightened. All my front and confidence were overwhelmed by the reality of the situation.

I remembered when my mum had once tried to talk me out of boxing. 'Have you ever thought about what else you might want to do?'

I hadn't. Until now, I'd never *needed* to consider anything else. Yesterday's Hamilton newspaper was on the table next to my bed, so I took a look. I turned the pages quickly without taking much in and stopped at the wanted ads. Gardener, window cleaner, chauffeur, barman, janitor, decorator, house cleaner, office cleaner, window cleaner, hairdresser, security guard, dog walker, medical secretary, computer analyst … it went on. There's even an advert for the police – they were recruiting. PC Dixon of Dock Green, don't think so. I smiled at the idea, thinking 'poacher turned gamekeeper', and skipped to the next section. Business opportunities, businesses for sale: pub, roadside café, warehouse, old peoples' home, etc. I doubted anyone would be looking for someone of my age – crippled and plastered – with a handful of GCSEs.

Fuck this. After browsing my options, my obsession to be world champion overtook me. I needed to leave this fucking awful place, where nothing happened. Every 24-hour day was like 600 hours of misery. Tam was asleep. I leant over and grabbed his crutches and laid them on my bed. I unplugged the plastic cannula taped on to my hand and removed it. I prised myself up, managed to get my legs off the bed and placed them on to the cold floor. I sat for a spell with my head spinning. I couldn't feel my feet or legs, which hadn't moved a muscle in a month. A month earlier, I'd been in a far worse situation, so I knew I could will myself, if I took it very, very slowly. One more step … one more inch at a time.

I grabbed Tam's crutches, planted them firmly on the floor with a bump, rose slowly up from the bed and stood up. The room swayed. I wobbled but stood fast. It felt like I'd taken a beating in the ring that didn't quite turn the lights out. It took me three minutes to get to the open door. I got two feet into the corridor, swaying like a distressed helicopter, when I saw my doctor walking towards me with his stooge. Just as I was losing my balance, they caught me and steadied me. They helped me back into the room and into bed. Tam was awake. 'I told you,' he said.

Doctor Wilson sat down in the chair beside my bed. 'It's time for physiotherapy. Where were you going?' he asked.

'Out for a stroll. Is there a chapel of rest in this fucking dump? I've got an old friend in there, and I need to have a chat. We need to talk about the good old days, and I need to ask him what it's like in heaven.' The doctor laughed a bit.

'One word of advice. Put your rehabilitation in first gear and imagine you are walking quickly, running, training, doing whatever you do, but if you overdo it at the start, you could end up being here even longer.'

Later that afternoon, I finished my first round of physiotherapy, which had gone at a snail's pace, but I was aching from the effort. The physios knew their stuff all right.

'We have a lot to do and have to take it slowly. Your muscles need to be rebuilt. It's a gradual process,' they said.

'How long do you mean?'

'You can't put a time on it. Every patient is different. A lot of successful rehabilitation has to do with your mind, though. You seem to be keen to get out of here, but we can't let you go until you are fully ready. Try to be patient. You'll know when you are ready.'

The next session was the next day, then every day after, including weekends. At first, I moved very slowly. I'd raise my arms and legs up and down while the physiotherapist applied gentle pressure. I had to build up muscles that were not just limp and weak but broken. 'Baby steps,' they'd say. Day by day, the baby steps turned into bigger, stronger steps until I could finally walk with the help of crutches. It was time to leave and face the void of uncertainly outside the hospital.

The last words the doctor said to me were still ringing in my ears when I walked out the door. 'It seems to me very unlikely that you will be able to box again. I'm sorry, Scott.

There has been so much damage to your leg and ankle, and you now have a plate in your arm. I wish you well.' I choked back tears, trying to put on a brave face, but those words were heart-breakers for me. Someone was telling me that my life was over. My mum had bought me a new white Adidas tracksuit to try to cheer me up a bit. She knew what I was thinking, even though we hadn't discussed the future.

'This will freshen you up,' she said.

Feeling totally not refreshed, I wore the tracksuit to leave the hospital. I didn't want anyone to see me on crutches. All they would see, in my mind, was a cripple. I wanted to be invisible. I had wanted to leave the hospital ever since I had arrived, but when I was actually leaving, I was dreading my departure. In the hospital, I had been well cared for and treated with respect. I hadn't had to think about a single thing. I had been cocooned. But now I was leaving and hobbling into a lot of uncertainty. What the fuck was I going to do?

We didn't go back to my mum's place. She'd lived there for 14 years but put it on the market while I was in the hospital. I would've been happy to have gone there, but it wasn't an option. So, we went straight to Papa's place. As always, unfailingly, Gran looked after me like I was a kid all over again. Love and care in bucket-loads and, as always, wonderfully proper homemade food. Chicken broth was her speciality, and her aim was to build me up. 'It's a miracle you are here, Scott. We must go to church as soon as you feel able.'

I put on a decent front but in the privacy of my own bedroom, demons invaded my head, asking me questions I couldn't answer. Is your life over? How about topping yourself? I was feeling really depressed and finding it hard to get out of bed until Papa came to the rescue.

'Come on, Scott. Get up. We're going out.'

I dragged myself out of bed, put on my white Adidas tracksuit and followed him on my crutches to his car. We drove around Hamilton for hours.

'Tell me if you see anyone you'd prefer not to see.'

With eyes peeled, I looked out for the two guys who attacked me with Garry McMillan. No luck. Papa drove me home.

'This isn't over until it's over, son. Mark my words.'

'Papa, let it go.' He glanced at me. His eyes told me that I shouldn't have said that. Papa never let anything go. He sorted it, oftentimes by silken threads.

It took a while, but I finally willed myself to get active. I needed to try to run, even if it was a very slow hop and wobble. My spirit was pushing me, and my body needed to respond. *Get up.* That voice again; the voice that saved my life. Enough of feeling sorry for myself, watching DVDs, laying low and twiddling my thumbs and doubts. I needed to test myself, if only to find out what I could and couldn't do.

I didn't want to be seen hobbling and maimed, so I waited until dusk. I wore a brace that was clipped on to my training shoe. Even running very slowly was an effort. I tried to run very slowly through Chatelherault Country Park, not far away, but kept falling over. It didn't matter; I kept getting up. As I gained confidence, I even started going out but always with a gang of very handy friends. I needed protection, if only not to feel so vulnerable and apprehensive. Looking back, I was still on edge and in shock.

For quite a few months, I went back to the hospital for physiotherapy: four times a week for the first month, then twice a month after that. Most of the work involved stretching and intense massages. I never missed a session. Something made me go without fail. At a very deep level, I wanted to get active and better.

Towards the end of physiotherapy, I was sitting in the hospital's waiting room when I spotted Nurse Rescue walking past the door. She looked upset. For some reason, she turned, saw me and came over.

'Hi Scott. Good to see you looking well.'

'You all okay, pet? You look like someone's died.'

'They have. Jim, just a wee laddie.' She pulled a white handkerchief from her pocket, blew her nose and wiped the tears from her eyes with the back of her hand.

'I'm sorry to hear it. You should take the day off.'

'I can't. I'm rushed off my feet. You know what it's like here.' I didn't know how these gals coped. There was no training for that.

Round 3

A Tragic Loss
Friday, 13 October 1995

I'd been training without distraction to get ready for my first professional fight in Glasgow. Fighting Drew Docherty for the British bantamweight championship, my pal Jim Murray was top of the bill. We'd been training together day and night at Big Alex Morrison's gym in Glasgow, then running miles through Strathclyde Country Park. Road running with someone else makes you step up the pace and clock more miles. After every session, Jim would go straight to the sauna to sweat out more weight. He was even chewing gum and spitting into a plastic bag, a good trick if you needed to lose every last ounce before a weigh-in. I remember thinking he was pushing himself too hard, but Jim was five years older than me and an inspiration, so I wasn't going to tell him anything. He was in the form of his life.

In my corner as always, Papa had been training me and I was in good nick, both physically and mentally. Jim had fought in 12 pro fights, so he was poised to take a shot at the title. This was my first pro fight and a big moment. It had been a long and hard road getting to this point on the map, and now I needed to prove myself. Although the fight was a big deal for me, the night was still Jim's.

I had just fought three good boxers in succession. Not all on the same day, thank God, but over a decent period of time. I had just enough time to regroup, reconsider, take stock and retune for the next event. Between the semi and the final, if you got there, you had a good slug of time, which was usually about a week, to prepare.

Papa had entered me into the senior flyweight Scottish Boxing Championships. I knew every entrant well. All good fighters and tough competition. There was Michael Crossan from Dennistoun in Glasgow, who had beaten everybody, Paul Shepherd from Edinburgh, a top boy nobody wanted to fight, as he was knocking everybody over, and western district champion John O'Mellon from the mining town of Croy. All three were older and more experienced than me. I'd just graduated from youth boxing, which was pitter-patter, slap-my-face kids' stuff by comparison. They must've thought I was there by an administrative cock-up.

We went to Meadowbank, where the eliminator was being held. Your first match was literally pot luck. Everyone's name went into a hat, everyone was weighed and then they gave you your draw for the day. Out of the three people I'd rather not have been fighting at all, I drew the name I particularly didn't want to see. John O'Mellon was a man with a full beard, chest hair and bulging muscles to prove it. By comparison, I looked like a skinny, shaved nun and I felt like it, too: vulnerable and out of my depth.

But, after the bell rang, I kept John at a distance and boxed his head off. I won all three rounds unanimously. In the quarter-finals, I drew Michael Crossan, a danger boy who'd won the Scottish championship three times in the last five years. By this time, he had chalked up 160 amateur fights. He liked to stand toe to toe and slug it out like a bulldozer with arms. The only way to fight him was by counter-punching on the back foot, which was something I was good at doing. It worked. I won all three rounds and people started taking notice. Who is this boy Dixon? I beat Thomas Walker in the semis. Honestly, I didn't know how he'd gotten this far in the competition. It must've been the luck of the draw for him. Now, I'd made it to the final match, and only Paul Shepherd stood between me and the championship cup.

There'd been a two-week gap between the semis and the final, and I must've let my diet slip. At the weigh-in, just three hours before the fight, I was overweight. We went into Edinburgh, put the sweats on, worked out and ran. I was still overweight, so did more work on the skipping ropes while chewing gum and spitting out the saliva. Papa towelled me dry real hard, and I just made the weight but was drained before the fight had even begun. Paul Shepherd beat me on points, got picked for the Commonwealth Games and went on to win the gold medal. It could've been me, but it didn't matter. What lay ahead for me tonight was a different kettle of fish altogether.

Pro boxing is a massive step up. Nobody can describe the difference unless they've done it themselves. While an amateur match may go for nine minutes (three rounds), a professional match may go for 12 gruelling three-minute rounds. That's 36 minutes of intense concentration and rapid, instinctive reaction with enough stamina in the tank. Even when the needle says empty, and your arms and legs feel like lead, you can't take your eye off the ball for a second or it's lights out.

On my debut pro appearance, I went the distance and beat Andrew Smith on points. I'd caught him with a few shots that should've knocked him over, but he was good and covered up well. I had a much bigger hit rate and every solid punch earned me another point to win another round. It was my first big victory, with half the crowd on my side and the other half on his, all cheering, booing, swearing and yelling advice or abuse. It can be more dangerous being in the crowd than in the ring, especially up in Scotland, where rivalry is deeply entrenched and rife. The fight was on Friday the 13th as well, so anything could've happened. I am a bit superstitious.

On the way back to my dressing room, after winning my first professional fight, I touched gloves with Jim and wished him good luck as he walked past me. I watched Jim and his ring men walk into the blinding spotlights as his Led Zeppelin entrance music was bursting the crowd's eardrums. I wasn't going to miss a second of this. I stripped off my kit, got changed and raced straight back to catch the action.

Jim put one glove on the ropes and vaulted square on to the canvas. His moment against Drew Docherty had arrived.

The MC lifted his microphone and his voice boomed out over the fading rock music. 'Ladies and gentlemen, the British bantamweight championship ...' The bell rang, and they squared up and touched gloves. The crowd went as mental as a crowd at a Rangers versus Celtic match, but the supporters here weren't segregated. If not during the fight, the scene would kick-off later. It was a powder keg with a short-fuse situation, and everyone was carrying a flame.

The fight was going Jim's way. The scorecards had him eight rounds in front. He'd got through two minutes and 40 seconds of the last round and seemed certain to win the belt when Docherty planted one straight, smack into his shoulder. Jim dropped to his hands and knees, rolled over, banged the canvas with his gloves three times, then laid completely still. It wasn't a shot good enough to put Jim down. There was something very wrong.

When he went down, the crowd kicked off. Bottles and chairs were flying, punches were thrown, and lock-back knives were pulled. The commotion prevented the medical boys from getting to the ring for at least three minutes. I managed to fight my way through the mayhem to get my mum, Papa and Gran, aunts and uncles, cousins and my girlfriend, Yvonne. I led them to the hotel's kitchen and bolted the door.

'Fucking hell!'

After everyone had left, and it was safe for us to leave, Gran was sitting on a kitchen chair looking stunned.

'Gran, my love, are you okay?'

'No, not really. This is much too much for me, Scott.'

I looked into her lovely blue eyes. 'Just sit here for as long as you want, then I'll take you home.'

'I always hoped you would do something else. One way or another, you are going to get hurt. I don't want to be here to see that.'

I rubbed my hands together not knowing what to say. As far as she was concerned, I was her son. I'd won that night, and that was a big moment for me, but I had also lost. Seeing Gran looking so bewildered and upset was a massive big leveller. It was something I just couldn't shake off.

Jim died two days later in intensive case having suffered a brain haemorrhage. The boxing world stopped still to take it all in. I was knocked sideways by the tragic loss of such a close friend, but I kept it deep inside me, not wanting to talk to anyone, not even Papa. Gran wouldn't talk about it and I knew why. That's when my doubts starting creeping in. My head was filled with voices chattering like magpies. Should I call it a day and pack it in? Everyone knows boxing is dangerous. Hundreds have died in the ring or soon afterwards. The statistics are chilling. It's not only the deaths, but also the brain damage. But until then, I hadn't known anyone close to me die because of boxing.

Jim's death brought about a boxing legacy. Bradley Stone had died at York Hall in London the year before. Frank Warren, Murray's promoter, established an overdue Murray Stone Foundation to finance MRI scans for every British fighter. Jim's bronze statue, bearing the words 'A young man who died in pursuit of his dreams', was unveiled in Newmaines the following year. To this day, nobody has spray-painted graffiti on it or stolen it for scrap. It would be the last thing anyone did if they were caught. Jim stands proud, upright and remembered forever as a true son of Scotland by friend and foe alike.

There had always been, and always will be, pressure to shut down or modify boxing in some way. Limiting blows to the head always seemed like a non-starter. The press was always full of it and seething when things went wrong. Looking back, I remember reading what was reported in the *Daily Mail* about the Paul Ingle and Mbulelo Botile fight in 2000. That was long after Jim died, but pressure to stop or apply damage limitation to boxing was always popping up like a jack-in-the-box. You couldn't stop it, just close it down for a while until someone else lifted the lid and let the truth out.

Speaking on Paul Ingle, 28 and now in critical condition, the *Daily Mail* wrote:

> The defeated champion was on the operating table at Sheffield's Royal Hallamshire Hospital within 45 minutes of his 12th round collapse, said promoter Frank Warren. Consultant neurosurgeon Robert Battersby, who carried out the operation to remove a blood clot from the fighter's brain, said he was 'making satisfactory progress'.
>
> He said: 'He is receiving expert care and his condition will continue to be monitored closely. Paul now needs time and space to recover from his traumatic injury.'

Labour MP for Newport West, Paul Flynn, said he intended to pursue his efforts to ban head blows. A Parliamentary Bill is expected next year. 'Boxing is unique in encouraging blows to the head,' he said. 'A boxer can receive hundreds of blows to the head in a single bout. One neurosurgeon has claimed that 80 per cent of all boxers have brain scarring as a result of the cumulative effects of blows.' He said the Bill was not seeking to ban boxing but to 'outlaw blows to the head in the same way that blows below the waist are banned now', allowing the sport to continue 'without the carnage'.

A spokeswoman also voiced the British Medical Association's long-standing opposition to the sport. 'The BMA finds it impossible to justify deliberately causing damage to the brain and the eye. The effects are cumulative so the more often you fight the more chance you have of being injured. We would ultimately like to see it banned but it will only happen if there's a change in the law and in public opinion. What we tend to see in cases like these is more people are turned off boxing and that's what it will take to see it banned,' she said.

Alex Morrison asked me to go to his Glasgow haulage and scrapyard, where people dumped crashed cars and anything metal for cash. It always struck me as being a tad ironic that he had a scrapheap, because that's where all boxers finish up sooner or later; it was merely a matter of time. He had an office on the ground floor and when Alex wanted to see you, make no mistake, you went. The rule of thumb was not to be late. Alex was one of the most on-time people on earth.

Big Alex *was* big. Eighteen stone packed into a 6ft 3in frame. He couldn't get suits off the peg, so he had a tailor who made them for him. His office was like a boxing memorabilia shop. Autographed boxing gloves hung from nails, a punch bag was propped up in the corner, and framed and signed fight photographs and posters filled nearly every inch of the red brick walls. There was also a massive oil painting he'd commissioned of Ali knocking out Liston. It was there to remind us what's possible when you boxed using your brains. On his desk was a photograph of Jim already in a frame waiting to be hung. Alex may be as tough as old leather boots, and nothing usually bothered him, but it looked like something had rattled his cage. His eyes were watering. He got straight to the point.

'Why did I ask you to come see me?'

'Jim,' I said, my eyes drifting to the photograph on his desk.

'How do you feel?'

'He was a true friend. He ...' I paused for breath and to steady myself.

'He what, Scott?'

'He gave me advice about everything.'

'We could all use advice sooner or later.'

'Even women; he told me just to ask them all, someone might say yes.' Alex raised the merest hint of a smile, then it faded. Now my eyes were watering.

'Do you want to carry on? If you don't, I understand, but you *do* have what it takes. You stick at it where others go down. But it's your decision.'

'I don't know.'

'Take two weeks off and think about it.' He handed me a stuffed envelope. 'We're square. Nobody's holding you. Whatever you decide, I respect.'

I heard later that Alex had asked all 20 boxers under his wing the same question. Maybe he had been thinking of packing it in, too. Reckon Alex was so massive, and Jim so wee by comparison, he must've thought of him as just a kid, like one of his own. Alex was a family man, born in a croft and bred on the Isle of Skye. That's a tough existence. Alex and Papa were a lot alike. They were both from a different era, when deep-entrenched values still existed along with miracles, scruples and diplomacy. Since then, things had gone awry.

Nothing nailed Alex like an interview I read in *The Sun* written by Matt Bendoris in 2010.

> Alex is one intimidating man in the flesh, with his
> big frame filling the cramped office next to his gym,
> where we meet in Glasgow's East End. But he can also
> be extremely charming and downright funny. He picks
> up a pair of boxing gloves from his heavy oak desk and
> quips: 'Got these for a bargain this morning. They're
> second hand but totally unused — they belonged to
> Audley Harrison.'

Alex's walls are lined with pictures of all the greats, from Muhammad Ali to Sugar Ray Leonard. But Audley, who was floored by David Haye in a controversial fight at the weekend, won't be joining them.

Alex also had to scrap his way to the top. Born and raised in a croft with his brother on the Isle of Skye, the family eked out an existence living off the land and only speaking in their native Gaelic. Alex says: 'I only learned English when a cousin from Glasgow came to stay with us after being evacuated during the war.'

He moved to Glasgow by himself at the age of 15 where he had his pocket picked on his first day in the city. It would be the last time somebody got one over on the big islander.

That was Alex through and through.

When cops are killed, police unite. Every cop knows it could happen to them, so when it does, they join ranks countrywide. After Jim's death, boxers put aside their political, religious, territorial and commercial differences and amassed as one great united force at Jim's funeral at Newmaines Protestant Church. A lot of Catholics turned up, too. Religions rubbing shoulders can start a fire, but I was praying that wouldn't happen today. This was too much of a leveller for anyone, no matter who they were or what they believed in. This was Jim's last outing. He'd thrown his last punch and was in a box way before his time.

On the day of Jim's funeral, I had to drag myself out of bed. Half of me wanted to stay under the covers, but I had to go. I wanted to go. I walked into the church wearing all the hallmarks of respect. A black suit, black tie, white shirt, cherry blossom-polished black shoes and Ray Bans. Whilst all that flashy front was me on the outside, it wasn't how I felt. I was lost inside it all and I couldn't believe it was happening. The church was without air or any ray of hope. I couldn't sit down because every seat was taken, so I stood at the back. Scanning the mass of dark-suited bodies, most of whom I knew, I took in the scene, felt dizzy and tried to ride it.

I opened my eyes. Papa was looking down at me flat on my back with familiar faces surrounding him, all staring at me. I felt nauseous and rolled over just in case I threw up. They helped me on to my feet and out into the fresh air. Jim's death had hit me harder than I'd let on, but I was devastated. I had lost my compass, my direction. I was at another crossroads with a head filled with questions without answers. Maybe I should've gone the football route and not boxing, but that dream of playing for the Rangers was now like a leaf that had fallen from a tree, landed in moving water and vanished from sight. It had already passed under the bridge with the current.

Next day, late morning, I went back to the church, which smelt of polish and extinguished candle-wax smoke. The door was open. All the altar silver had been stolen years ago, so there was nothing else to take, save the lead on the roof. I was alone, just me with me. I sank to my knees on the front pew and closed my eyes. I was being tested. It wasn't *only* because Jim had died. I was in the shadows and something was coming to get me. I was standing at a crossroads with four ways to go: forwards, backwards, left or right. The question was which road led to a home and some kind of happiness. Who am I and what am I doing? Am I going to Damascus or Mandalay?

I lost myself in the ether of this place of rest, where lost souls came to pray for forgiveness and mercy. They came because they had nowhere else to go. They were deserted, cast aside with nobody good crossing the road for them. It was also a place where people congregated and sang, got married, buried and christened. I was christened Scott Edward Semple here. No way did I want to be a Semple, my father's name. I changed my name to Scott Dixon when I was 16. I stopped thinking, allowing the silence to absorb me.

A few minutes later, a loud noise snapped me back to my mind, a place I was trying to depart. Someone had switched on a Hoover that yelled like it was choking on its innards. Jesus Christ! Is there no peace? I rose up, left the few flickering candles of remembrance and stepped into a thankless day of falling rain. The day was covered over with a shroud of grey sky that reached right up into the heavens. I looked upwards. Help me, please. I was at the lowest point in my life. I didn't know if this was grief or depression or both. Grief is understandable, and I knew that everyone had to experience that at some point, but clinical depression is Satan's dark, confusing and debilitating invention.

Just when I thought all was lost, and my game was finally over, Rocky Balboa and Sugar Ray Robinson stepped in to rescue me. I glued myself to *Rocky* films, watching them over and over again like a movie addict. They helped me to find my feet and get back on them. Robinson's story *Pound for Pound* was an eye-opener, highlighting fights against Jake LaMotta, Gene Fullmer, Rocky Graziano and Kid Gavilan to name but a few. Robinson had 174 wins with 109 knockouts. 'Hurting people is my business' and 'I'll quit when I start to slide' were just two of his legendary quotes. Stopping, rewinding, watching the action again in slow motion and imagining I was in his boots, I studied the fights. I loved his flamboyance. Dodging and weaving, he was a master of avoidance and could punch. He had plenty to show me. Sluggers like Tyson and Marciano fought in a way that I didn't. Not sure they were what I'd call boxers, but they were definitely great fighters. Feeling reloaded, I went back to the gym and got stuck in.

Round 4

London

1998

Boxing is a lot about timing – as is life. For a while, Papa had been talking to me about going to London. 'If you're going to move up, you need to move on,' he said. 'London's got better training, better sparring partners and better opportunities. If you're going to get recognition, you need to spend time down south. I've got connections.'

'Are you coming with me?'

'Yes, if you want, son. But you're a bit like a cat ready to walk alone.' Papa was right. I *was* finally ready for a change of scene. My contract had expired with Alex Morrison, so I took the opportunity. Otherwise, I reckoned there would've been hell to pay. Nobody ever walked out on Alex.

Me and Papa went to London to nose around the gyms in the East End. We first met matchmaker and trainer Dean Powell at the Fitzroy Lodge Boxing Club. He wanted to see what I could do. Five minutes later, I was sparring with Charlie Rumble, who was handy, but I dominated him, bashing him all over the place. Dean appeared with paper and pen.

'If you sign this contract, I'll make sure we go places.'

Papa took me to one side. 'Don't sign anything yet. There's more to London than just this place.' I rarely argued with him.

'I'm gonna be here for a few days. Let me think about it,' I told Dean.

The next day, Papa was meeting some old boxing friends in Soho, so I headed off to the Peacock Gym in Caxton Street North in Canning Town. A bit of a rundown shithole of an area, with boarded-up houses, shops with metal bars on the windows, vagrants sitting on doorsteps, alleyway cats and dogs wandering about, and not one estate agent office in sight, Canning Town was a definite no-go area for the middle class. There was a noticeable absence of banks, post offices or any place worth holding up. It was nothing like *EastEnders*, which was pretty classy by comparison.

Like the area, the Peacock Gym was in a state of total disrepair. Boxes of trash were everywhere, and dank light struggled to shine through its smashed, dirty windows. The gym looked like it hadn't seen a broom or a lick of paint in decades. That said, two flashy Porsches were parked outside on the pavement, with parking tickets stuck under the window wipers. I figured they were probably nicked, but what did I know?

The gym's damp walls still had water running down them, making brown puddles on the concrete floor, and it stank of sweat and filth, but it was buzzing like a beehive in the heat of summer with boxers and trainers. It was a busy place, with quite a few young women in there, too. I immediately noticed one woman in particular but decided to stick to the business in hand. The gym had two boxing rings, plenty of punch bags and all the gear you needed. It looked promising in spite of first appearances. Also, it was the sort of dump that I felt at home in.

Suddenly, I felt a wave a doubt. What the fuck did I offer? At the time, I had 18 unbeaten professional fights under my belt, a few hundred quid in my pocket, my kit bag, the *will* to win and the *need to* make something of myself. Before signing anything or doing anything, I needed to stash any doubts under the carpet and stamp them to death. I had enough to offer.

I'd heard of the Bowers brothers because word travels, but I had no idea if they'd heard of me. While taking in the sights and smells of the gym, a big guy with hands the size of hams walked over to me, extending one of those hams.

'I'm Tony. Welcome to my palace.'

I held my hand out. He could've wrapped his around mine twice. We shook.

'Scott Dixon,' I said.

'What can we do for each other?' Tony asked.

'I'm down from Hamilton looking for a gym.'

He whistled through the gap in his front teeth like he was hailing a cab, then a guy appeared dressed ready to step into the ring. 'Paul, I wanna see you work with Scott.' Two other fellers joined Tony to watch. I did a quick job on Paul, knocking him over twice inside two minutes. 'Scott, get changed and meet us across the road at the pub.'

The pub door had a poster taped on to the glass window. Chas and Dave were playing there that night. They were Cockneys going places in the charts with a big following. I sat down with the brothers, Tony and Martin.

'You were one of Morrison's men? Left his stable on good terms?' Martin asked.

'Yes.'

'We were sorry to hear about Jim. We sent our respects,' said Tony.

I nodded.

'One of our fighters just had a brain scan because of him,' Tony added.

'He didn't die for nothing then,' I said.

'So, how many pro fights have you clocked?' asked Martin.

'Eighteen.'

'Losses?'

'None.'

'I've seen you in action and I've made some calls before. I can think of a better name for you. There's a gap in the game for this one,' Martin said.

'Oh yeah?' I was fighting under the name Toby Dixon at the time. Martin leaned back a bit with a hint of excitement.

'Super Scott Dixon. Superman theme music. Superman colours on your shorts and boots. What do you say?'

I didn't want to drop my grandfather's name without thinking about it, but this new name idea rang bells loud and clear. Why not? 'Yeah,' I smiled. 'Great.'

Over steak and chips, fresh orange juice (I wasn't going to touch booze in case they got the wrong idea about me) and real coffee, we agreed terms and shook hands. The Bowers also owned the pub. They gave me a kitted-out apartment upstairs, a Mazda MX5 and £200 a week. I'd never been paid regular wages before. The Bowers were treating me like family. I didn't even ask myself or Papa why.

Big hands Tony was nicknamed Tony Soprano. He ran the show in a cool, calm way, but there was also a 'make no mistake, I'm the boss here and don't ever forget it' element to how he operated. Martin was more reserved. Less vocal although not always, he was usually found in the gym working out. He was more cunning and unpredictable. He could appear all placid and then suddenly strike. Paul, the youngest, was always up to mischief, a typical Cockney villain. Big smiles that hid motive was something they all had in common. You didn't want to cross any one of them, let alone all three.

Along with the brothers, Uncle Jackie Bowers was always in the background (or the foreground when the situation called for it). Jackie was a great trainer with an inside-out knowledge of the game, who'd seen and done it himself. He was a lot like my grandfather in terms of experience, history and acumen. Of his many claims to fame, Jackie had once beaten Terry Spinks but that was when they were kids. Jackie had also helped Terry Lawless build one of the best stables in British boxing history.

Dog's balls were the only way to describe the Peacock Gym. You couldn't help but notice the gold Rolex watches, the Porsches, the snappy suits, the tarts and the celebs at the gym. Boxers and the matches make very little. That is, unless you managed, promoted and match-fixed fights. Most boxers get paid in tickets to start off.

Say you get 2,000 tickets and sell 1,000, then you spend the money like I've done. What do you do with the other 1,000 tickets? Owe, maybe. That's why it's good to be on a winning streak. After you win a title, you'll have some say. You can help choose and properly negotiate your next contest. At that point, you'll also have something to tuck away for a rainy day, which always comes. There isn't a lot of sun in boxing and when you're finished, it stays cloudy after the very last count.

The Bowers were definitely fans of boxing. They meant it, loved it and breathed it, and that's why I worked with them initially. But there was always a whiff of something else going on. Late at night, in their head office, people turned up unexpectedly, blinds were shut, and doors were locked. There was always another agenda. You could feel it. Everybody saw it happening, but nobody spoke about it – no way.

Every now and then, the Old Bill would drop in, pretending it was a social call. They never had search warrants or any reason to be there, but the brothers put up with the inconveniences. While I trained, the cops hung about in the street, sniffed around, stopped people and took the occasional person in for questioning. More than open surveillance, it was more like they wanted to be seen doing it, maybe to cover up the real surveillance that *was* happening or being planned. Regardless, the Bowers were in their sights.

One night at the Peacock pub, the Bowers got up and left without paying. I went upstairs to my apartment, which wasn't what I expected after the first-day meeting. It was a fully furnished apartment with a kitchen, bathroom with shower, a big telly, carpets and curtains. After walking around the place, I looked out of the window to see Paul drive off in a black Porsche, rocketing into the distance, going straight through a red light. I wanted some of that. There had to be an easier way to make money other than just boxing.

With every passing day, I felt myself morphing into one of them. They were lining up some good fights, and we all got on well. We'd go out together and, no doubt, they were looking after me without asking for anything in return, other than a win or two.

I'd finished training and nipped upstairs to see Tony, who was still in his office. I tapped on the door, waited for his reply, and entered.

'Everything all right, Scott?'

'Yeah, thanks. I wanted to thank you for everything.' I hesitated for a moment, but asked, 'Can I do anything for you?' He looked me in the eyes, squeezed his hand into his inside suit pocket and handed me a piece of paper. Written on it was a name and address. 'This geezer owes me ten grand.'

That was the first time in my life I'd be a debt collector. I didn't know how to do it but knew it needed to be done smart. No comeback or fuss or blood or bullets; just a smooth and quick operation.

They'd done so much for me. It was the least I could do for them.

I needed a jaw-dropper. I needed a guy who looked so menacing that anyone in their right mind would do the necessary – cave in and hand over. Frankie Armitage, who we called Army because he looked like a whole army platoon, was that jaw-dropper. Army was like a massive, lovely and goofy version of the actor Bernard Bresslaw, who starred in the *Carry On* films that my gran adored. Bernard stood 6ft 7in. If you put sunglasses on Bernard, you got Army. I knew where to find him. Playing dominoes in the Peacock pub, Army was sitting in the far corner of the pub on his own. I sat down next to him.

'Hello, pal, how are ya?' Army looked at me.

'Oh hey, Scott. Wanna play a game?' he asked, opening a cardboard box of dominoes.

'Yeah, a bit later. Wanna make a hundred quid for 30 minutes' work?'

'What for?'

'Nothing really. Just be yourself and don't smile. And keep your shades on.'

'Do I look alright for the job in this clobber?' He was wearing a massive pair of overalls splashed with red paint.

'You look perfect, mate.'

Army squeezed himself into the passenger seat of my car. He shoved the seat back to the maximum and his legs still bent double like triangles. We arrived at the destination: a house with all its lights on. The noise filtering out into the street told me there was a party going on. With Army standing nearby, but out of sight, I rang the doorbell. Nothing happened, so I pressed it again without taking my finger off the button. Eventually a guy opened the door.

'Mike?' I asked.

'Yeah,' he replied.

'Tony Bowers sent me to collect.'

'Oh yeah?' he said, smiling sarcastically. 'He sent a kid to do a man's job, did he?'

Army was in the shadows, so he hadn't seen him yet. On cue, Army stepped in to the porch light, waving his arms. He looked less like Bernard Bresslaw and more like Frankenstein. Mike's face dropped. I was hoping Army didn't ask Mike for a game of dominoes. 'I want it now or we're coming in. I promise you, we will fuck you up and your party. You've got two minutes.' Mike disappeared inside but left the door open.

Army and I stood waiting in the hallway. Paying no attention to us, people were moving from room to room. Mike came back and handed me a large envelope.

'I hope it's all there,' I said, looking inside.

'It's there,' he replied nervously.

'Better had be or we'll be back.'

'Was I alright? Was that what you wanted?' Army asked on the drive back to the pub.

'You have no idea, pal. You were absolutely fucking perfect,' I laughed.

I gave Army 100 quid in tens, and he made his way back to his table in the corner.

'Ta Scott. Want a game of doms now?'

'Yeah, in a minute. Grab me a pint.'

I walked upstairs and dropped ten wads of notes held tight with rubber bands on to Tony's desk. 'That was quick,' he said. After looking in the envelope, Tony handed me a grand and a set of car keys with a leather Porsche badge attached to it. 'I'm away with the wife and family for a week. Don't scratch it.'

I went back downstairs for a game of dominoes, a pint and to give Army another 50 quid. 'Oh, ta very much Scott,' he said, pocketing the cash. 'This is a bit like winning the pools.' Whilst Army was a massive, towering figure, he was pretty much harmless. One time, Army was so pissed he accidently fell on someone sitting at a table in the pub and messed him up pretty bad. By chance, the guy had slapped his woman earlier and made her cry. People thought Army 'attacked' him to teach the guy a lesson. He hadn't. Since then, everyone who didn't know Army tended to avoid him. Part of me felt bad for him.

After a while, I started moving small quantities of weed and charlie to make easy money. I knew people who were always looking for supply. The best place to turn drugs into quick cash was in Soho. I'd drop off small deliveries at night to a guy called Jacko in Soho Square. I'd drive around the square a few times until he flashed his headlights. Easy enough but violence was always in the air. Jacko soon vanished off the face of the earth, so I did what little dealing I could closer to where I lived.

The drug thing wasn't new. I came from a rundown council estate, so we did what we could to earn a little. Growing up, you learned you could make a little doing either this or that, so everybody did *that*. It wasn't the exception; it was the rule. Even though I was an athlete, I did have some very naughty mates, and drugs were always an option if I needed to turn a pound note. For a while, I ran with football hooligans when raves and ecstasy exploded. Pills were going for £15 each and we could get them for £5, which made for good, quick dough.

Martin's son, Tony, was celebrating his birthday at Beckton ski slopes outside Canning Town and we were all invited. I was dating a real beauty at the time, and it was probably love. I hadn't strayed since we'd been together. Like love-dumb teenagers, we were holding hands, having quiet meals and making love instead of fucking. Not long before, she had walked into the Peacock Gym and into my life. She was a long-haul air hostess for one of the big airlines and probably got the job on her looks alone. She was about 5ft 5in tall without shoes, lovely auburn hair, hazel eyes and a very tuned, athletic body.

She hired me as a personal trainer but turned up to the first session with her dad. Her dad was a cool customer and wary. It took me a fair wee while to break the ice with him. After our second training session, when he wasn't in my face, I asked her out and that was that. She had a very lyrical, faintly Irish accent and was funny. She had a whole headful of hilarious jokes, most of them about the way the Irish see things. There's one I've never forgotten.

An Irish guy was trimming the hedge in front of his house while his wife was sweeping up the cuttings. Two young hitchhikers with backpacks, a young man and a young woman, approached him looking very tired.

'Hello,' the young man said. 'Can you help us, please?'

'To be sure to be sure. I will if I can, and if I can't, I'll wish that I could,' he smiled.

'How far is it to Ballyvourney?'

'It's a lovely spot and not far, just over the hill.'

'Thank you.'

'Cheerio. And top of the morning to you.'

After the hitchhikers were out of sight and sound, his wife looked at him.

'Why did you say Ballyvourney was not far, when it's 25 miles away?'

'Oh, because they looked so tired.'

That summed up the Irish – daft as brushes. They just see things differently.

I was at Tony's birthday party having a drink, and the beauty was on the dance floor. She was such a great mover. I noticed a guy in the corner staring at me and telegraphing a look I didn't like. Next thing, he was in my face. I shook my head and blew air through compressed lips.

'Who are you looking at?' he snarled. Jesus, not again. Why me all the time?

'Hey mate, ease up. It's a party. Have a drink.'

His right hand was clenching a pint glass with jagged edges, so he'd already broken it. With a wide Glasgow smile, which these idiots always wore, he lunged to cut me, but it was very bad timing. She must've seen what was happening and walked up to me the moment he tried to stick the glass in my face. She put her hand up, and the shards cut the artery on her wrist. While blood spurted out like a geyser, I cut the guy a shot and he went down cold. She started screaming and the music stopped. I ripped off my shirt, wrapped it around her hand and gripped her arm just above the elbow.

'Get out the fucking way!' I yelled. I carried her to my car with the help of a complete stranger and drove like a maniac to London Orbital Hospital. She had an emergency operation and stayed overnight. I was seething with anger; one second away from going fucking thermo-nuclear ballistic. Once she was settled in hospital, I phoned her employer to tell them what had happened, then called Martin to fill him in. 'Leave it to me, Scott,' he said. 'I'll get back to you.'

He rounded up Tony and Paul. We met the next morning at 8am at a greasy spoon on Barking Road near Upton Park. Tony had made a call and knew who this guy was. We climbed into his immaculate, racing-green 60s Jag. He'd taken it in lieu of an outstanding debt. Danny Hunt, my target, didn't live far away. We pulled up outside a block of flats. I opened the rear car door, hell-bent on getting on with this, got one leg out and Tony stopped me in my tracks.

'No, Scott. We're going in, he's coming out, and you're gonna have a straightener in the street. No discussion.'

I stayed in the back with Roy Hilder, who had come along for the ride. I watched them open the door to the building and saw them disappear up the stairs as the glass door slowly closed. I got a replay from Tony later on. Tony had banged on the door. A timid woman opened it.

'Danny's here, yes?'

'Err ...'

'Tell him, he's coming out or we're coming in. He hurt a woman last night. She was badly cut up and hysterical. It won't do.'

On the way down the stairs with Danny, Tony put it to him this way. 'Take the line of least resistance, Danny. Say to Scott, "I'm sorry, it was a terrible mistake. Please, let's shake hands."' As they came through the door, I was waiting, hell-bent on revenge. Danny was holding his hand out, looking like he wanted to make peace the easy way. Boom, down he went. Martin stepped in.

'Scott, that's it. It's finished,' he said sharply. That's it? Now I wanted to fight everyone. Tony cooled me down, putting his hand on my shoulder.

'Let's go for a stroll. I need to get something.'

We walked about 100 yards to a corner shop. Tony pulled out a 20 and bought two bunches of red roses. We went back to the Jag and waited while he went into the building. When he came back, he told us he'd gone upstairs to give Danny's mum the flowers. The Bowers had two sides to their coin.

They were gentlemen, always respectful, courteous and kind to many, especially women, both young and old.

'Manners maketh the man,' Gran always said.

On 19 September 1998, I tasted defeat for the first time to Michael Carruth on his home turf at the National Basketball Arena in Dublin. Trained by Steve Collins, Carruth was one of the best fighters Ireland had produced in years. He had also won an Olympic gold medal in Barcelona in 1992. But with Jackie Bowers, Martin and Papa on my side, I had equal, if not better, training and support.

Michael Carruth had also lost his last fight on a majority decision against the German fighter Michael Loewe, who took the WBO title by just one point. German boxing at the time was never straightforward. You had to knock someone out twice to get a win in Germany. Carruth probably did win that fight; it just wasn't going to show in the record books. I knew the loss would be on his mind. A loss always is, and there's no getting away from it, but a good team can help you move forward.

We were staying at Jurys Inn on the northern flank of the River Liffey. The hotel was bursting with Irish supporting Carruth. That's the beauty of the Irish. They unite to give a whole nation's worth of support, whether it's boxing, rugby, football or anything else. By contrast, one Scottish fella came up to me and wished me luck.

The stadium was jam-packed full of 10,000 Irish all singing 'Danny Boy'. It was mental. I put my hand on the ropes and vaulted into the ring. Everyone booed me while waiting for their boy. Steve Collins was in Carruth's corner winding up the crowds. Steve was one of them, of course, and so fucking Irish that he should've had green skin and Shamrocks for hands. My boys were all wearing their Peacock t-shirts, and Jackie was wearing one of those crazy Scottish 'See you Jimmy' hats with orange hair hanging down the back. He looked like a complete nutcase. The sight of an old Cockney guy with a bashed-up face, a ridiculously mad hat and Peacock t-shirt was priceless.

Ding! After the first round, I was doing pretty good. In the second, I caught him with a massive left hook and he dropped to his knees. Immediately, I went to the furthest neutral corner of the ring. After about ten seconds, I watched Carruth get up and wobble, but the ref didn't give a count. The bell rang.

I sat down on the stool and Papa went to work: wet sponge on my face with one hand, gum shield removed with the other, wet towel on my neck, a dry towel pats me off, grease on the eyebrows and under my eyes and a 'good luck' pat on the back. It was all perfectly synchronised like a Formula One pit stop. Nobody did it better than Papa.

'You're gonna have to knock this cunt out,' Jackie yelled.

'I know.'

After six more rounds of trading, I caught him in the ninth again. Just like in the second round, he dropped without a count from the referee. What the fuck was going on? Although Carruth was getting in some good body shots and earning points, he kept walking into everything I was throwing. In the 11th round, I caught him proper with a great body shot and he fell over. Again, there was no count. Instead, the ref docked me a point for a low blow. When it was finally over, it went to the scorecards. I lost 117-116.

After the decision was made by the judges, there was nothing anyone could do to change it. Only the sports journalists and commentators could have their say. It was my first loss, my first stain on an otherwise clean sheet. After the defeat, I became depressed as hell. I went back to Scotland and spent a week in bed, not wanting to see or talk to anyone. Nothing interested me, not even birds. It wasn't going to last forever but it took me a while to digest the loss.

In March of 1999, we decided to organise an outing to watch Lennox Lewis fight Evander Holyfield at Madison Square Garden. It was a big fight, a massive occasion and another scale of boxing altogether. I'd never been to New York but had won a few fights in succession, so I was flush for once. It was the perfect opportunity to take Papa along for the ride. Me, the Peacock gang, Freddie and Jamie Foreman, and some of the Glasgow mob – old Franco and Albert – were quite a formidable assembly on one jet aircraft, and we all flew first class. Tommy Wisbey, who had a thing for trains, and Tommy Moffitt were going to be with us at the fight. To amuse my Papa, we decided to get him a suit to fit the occasion.

When Frank Maloney appeared at fights, he used to wear a sequin suit. Well, we could do better than that and did. I got Papa's measurements from Gran and told her not to breathe a word to Papa. Tony Bowers' tailor did the rest. He made a Union Jack suit with sequins, while we got a white shirt, white shoes and a Union Jack tie. It was priceless. There was a showman hidden away in Papa who rarely raised his head, only two or three times as I remember. But for this trip, it was showtime!

Papa and I had never flown first class. It was a great experience. The booze and service both flowed non-stop. I'd never taken much to flying but could've got used to that first-class stuff. I almost forgot I was on a plane.

'This is the only way to travel, son,' Papa said. 'I think I'll have a nap.'

For me, New York was a jaw-dropper. You see it looming when you come over the Brooklyn Bridge, but when you're in it, you feel it. I was overwhelmed with the scale, the pace and the racket of the place. If everyone blew their car horns at once, you'd go deaf. I loved the coffee shops, the delis and their American breakfasts. I'm not a massive eater but how could anyone not get stuck into pancakes smothered in maple syrup? I also loved the way New Yorkers ordered breakfast: 'eggs over easy', just like in the movies.

We were all booked into The Plaza on Central Park, which looked more like a monument than a hotel. It was huge and extremely stylish in a 1920s kind of way. On the first night, we all went to Vito's Restaurant in Little Italy. A friend of Tony's was picking up the dinner tab. On the way there, Papa sang loudly while taking in the sights. 'New York, New York!' He stopped singing and looked sideways at me.

'I feel a wee bit guilty,' he said.

'What for?'

'Your Gran should be here, that's why. Did you know that Liza Minnelli, Andy Williams and Peggy Lee all sang in the Persian Room at our hotel? A photo of Liza Minnelli is hanging on my bedroom wall. You'd better explain *that* to Gran. The Beatles stayed here, too, when they first got to America.'

'Is John Lennon hanging on your wall as well? Papa, just enjoy. Gran would be happy to see you happy.'

Vito's Restaurant was unlike anywhere Papa and I had ever been. It was pure Italian, through and through. Big Mike welcomed us, seated us and made a fuss over us throughout the evening. He wouldn't let any of us order food, not even the wine.

'You are my guests, allow me to feed you. If I bring you something you don't like, just tell me and I'll bring you something else.'

We had baked aubergine with tomatoes smothered in soft cheese, an incredible meat dish and a delicious pudding served in a tall glass that you ate with a long spoon. After the meal, Big Mike brought a tray of little glasses filled with liquid. Coffee beans floated on the surface. He lit a match and ignited the top. 'Wait until they have burned for a while, then blow them out. Let it cool, then sip.'

Tony began to get up from the table. Before he could, Papa spoke to him.

'Tony, let me give you some money for this,' he said quietly.

'Certainly not,' he said. 'Everything in New York is on the house, Toby. You got the keys to the city. As long as you enjoy, that's all that matters.'

'Heya, Tony,' Papa said, doing a poor but passable imitation of an Italian-American accent. 'Bellissimo! Fantastico!' Everyone laughed. Did Papa enjoy it? For years, Papa would talk about *the* meal in Little Italy.

The next day, about an hour before leaving for the fight, we were all sitting in the hotel bar when Papa appeared. He was smartly dressed for a Glasgow night out, but not a New York one. It just wasn't flashy enough. I handed him a large, white cardboard box with our names written on the lid.

'We've got this for you, Papa, just to mark the occasion,' I said. He opened the box and took out the sequin suit, shoes, shirt and tie. His face lit up like a beacon.

'Well, I'll be ...' he said, looking the suit over. 'I'll be back in ten minutes.'

As he walked to the elevator, I could hear him laughing. When he came back, everyone in the bar stared at him. He was obviously a celebrity. He loved it and wouldn't sit down for fear of creasing it.

'I feel like Billy Smart.'

'Smarter,' said Martin, handing him a shot of single malt.

'Your health, everyone,' Papa toasted. 'I'm cock-a-hoop with this outfit. Thank you.'

'Toby, tonight you will upstage the event. You are the business and always have been,' said Tony. 'I salute you.'

Three yellow taxi cabs dropped us off about 500 yards from the Garden. On the street, Papa was the main attraction. Cars slowed to look, folks snapped photos, and gals on the sidewalk stopped to talk to him. A few wanted his autograph.

'Hey, Papa, do you want to swap jackets for a wee while?' He smiled at me.

'You having trouble landing girls, Scott? This is my jacket, so leave it out, will ya?'

The noise in the Garden was manic and deafening, and the occasion was very Yankee-doodle swanky. Everything was so over the top. I hadn't experienced anything like it. When the main event started, Lewis and Holyfield didn't just throw punches. They launched sledgehammers, jackhammers, bullets and missiles. It was a draw and a hard match to call, but a British judge fucked it up. Otherwise, it would have been Lewis's fight. I've always been sceptical about fights that end in a draw. For me, there was always a winner, no matter how tight the margin.

It was great watching Lewis in action. We also met him, and he remembered me from the days when he trained at the Peacock Gym. He was also a believer. 'The Lord certainly blessed you with the gift of fighting,' Lewis had said to me once. 'Every time you step into the ring, give Him ten seconds of your gratefulness for blessing you, and your path will always be clear to reach your goal.'

A lot of people in boxing shared a spiritual faith. When Jimmy Tibbs trained Nigel Benn at the Peacock, he always preached while working Benn on the pads. 'The Lord gave you this fabulous gift, so take it before He gives it to another fighter. Right, left, upper, now jab, jab, jab, faster. Come on! The Lord gave you this fabulous gift, so take it …' Jimmy would repeat.

Like Jimmy, a lot of other top cornermen believed in the Lord. This added to my faith. The seed planted in me at Sunday school continued to grow and flower around the ring. There was even a boxer's prayer, written by Tom Knight, which I used to recite. 'Ask you not for victory, for somehow that seems wrong …' I've never questioned the relationship between religion and a violent sport. One day, maybe, I'll take the time.

Next morning, Papa and I hailed a cab and went to Gleason's Gym in Brooklyn. Gleason's was not just holy ground for boxing, it was a cathedral studded with decades of boxing history. Open the door and straight away you're walking in the footsteps of the greats. Martin Scorsese also shot *Raging Bull* scenes here and his framed signed photographs were hanging on the walls. Me and Papa watched a guy working out for a bit. His body looked like hardened leather. I nudged Papa. 'You know who that is?' Papa nodded.

'It's poetry in motion, Scott. We don't do stuff like this back home. It's on another level.'

Suspended punch balls are usually the size of a football. In awe, me and Papa watched welterweight megastar Zab Judah work on a ball no bigger than a tennis ball. Judah hit it maybe 100 times without missing. If this was target practice, he must've had cross-wires in both eyes. He finished and walked off, so I gave it a shot. I landed the first one but missed with the second and third. This was something else. This was about pinpoint accuracy.

'We should get one of these and keep quiet about it,' I said.

'I'll get you a golf ball-sized one,' smiled Papa. 'Have to confess, I've not seen that before. Good thing you're not fighting him at any weight, or you might just have a problem.'

There was a quote by Virgil painted in black on a red wall. 'Now whoever has courage and a strong and collected spirit in his breast, let him come forward, lace on the gloves and put up his hands.' The phrase summed up boxing very neatly for me. Nobody has the faintest notion what it's really like. They can only imagine it. Until you're in the ring, where there is no way out, no going back or turning your back, it's hard to explain.

Round 5

Seeing Stars

March 1999

Paul McGuigan called Tony Bowers about assisting him with his new film, *Gangster No. 1*. Malcolm McDowell was playing the Soho crime lord, Paul Bettany. Paul asked Tony if he knew any boxers who'd be on for some *real* fight action. He wanted it real. He also told Tony he'd be using real criminals. Tony suggested me and Karim Bouali for the fight action. Paul also asked if Papa would be interested.

'Dunno, I'll ask him. Toby's not a criminal. Otherwise, he fits the bill massive. There's nothing about boxing he don't know.'

During a full filming day, me and the French-Algerian fought – for real. He couldn't speak English and must've thought it was a real fight, which it turned out to be. Every time the director shouted 'cut', Bouali treated it like the end of a round. In total, we shot 18 three-minute rounds. That's a lot of full-on boxing. The whole fight crew were proper criminals, and Roy Hilder was the referee. Maybe not surprising, given the casting, I did get robbed during filming. Movie opportunities were a bit like London buses. There was never one when you needed one, then two would come along pretty well at once.

In October 1999, I had my first big fight under the name 'Super' Scott Dixon. My opponent, the opposite of a pushover, was Derek 'The Rebel' Roche. Originally from Wexford in Ireland, but now fighting out of Leeds, he looked fearsome and had a spotless record. Undefeated in 21 fights and the current British welterweight champion, Roche only needed one more successful defence of the coveted Lord Lonsdale Challenge Belt to become its outright owner. I was going to do my best to make sure that didn't happen. I had spent 18 weeks training, the longest time ever in my life. Some of it was determination, but the fight date also kept getting pushed back. It had taken weeks to nail the date down in ink.

We decided to go to Coventry mob-handed. We met up at the Peacock Gym first, then went off in convoy in two big Jags. It was Martin and Tony Bowers, Old Jackie Bowers, Paul Lawson, Roy Hilder, Papa and me. It was a bit of an outing with seven of us. Some doubts did creep in on the way. Had I overtrained? Had I overdone it? If everyone thought I needed this much support, was there a problem ahead? I had to consciously stomp out these doubts. Like a wave, the doubts – and my conscious effort to erase them – became fuel. I suddenly felt good, determined and hell-bent on winning. We arrived at Coombe Abbey Hotel when Martin said something

I didn't understand at first. 'Your kinda place this, Scott. You'll love it here,' he laughed.

Reputed to be haunted, Coombe Abbey Hotel was a massive, repurposed monastery with 500 acres of parkland. It was spooky. Some old bugger in the distant past, who had owned the place, had a green-eyed stable hand named Matilda. Apparently, her child died, then she was sent packing. But before she left, Matilda cast a spell on the place. There was also a ghost named Geoffrey, who was murdered in 1345. Geoffrey wandered the corridors at night. Also, the kitchen regularly clattered with pots and pans as invisible hands hurled them around. Refusing to pay the bill, lots of guests had fled their rooms in the night, driven off with ashen faces and horrified expressions.

The Bowers kept telling me stories while we checked in: unexplained draughts, slamming doors, tapping on walls and spine-tingling presences. Fuck this, I don't do haunted hotels. I don't even watch scary films. I bet Martin booked it. He knew how much this kind of shit put the wind up me. He was always making cracks about it. I then noticed the receptionist had green eyes, but she seemed pretty friendly. Maybe her name was Matilda. Just for once, I didn't think I'd bother finding out. To make matters worse, we were booked for two nights, with an option of booking another hotel on fight night if we didn't feel like driving back to London. I knew I wouldn't get a wink of sleep.

My room was dark and badly lit, which made it all the spookier. I didn't bother unpacking. I just took what I needed out of my holdall. I borrowed a couple of silver candlesticks from the upstairs landing then called the front desk and asked them to send up some more candles and electric lamps. I lit the candles but they blew out. I tried again, same thing. Bollocks to this. I went downstairs to the bar, even though Jackie told me to stay away. On the way down the staircase, a black cat with yellow eyes stared at me. If they'd wanted me to be sensible, they should've booked me at a Travelodge. This place was dead abnormal.

The day before the fight, the weigh-in was electrifying. It was like *Deliverance* meets *Goodfellas*. Roche came in with his camp, all dressed in checked shirts and old denims that you wouldn't give to Oxfam. They looked a bit shambolic compared to us in our Hugo Boss suits, Prada shoes and Rolex watches. I took the upper hand at the weigh-in. I assured the press and the Sky Box Office people that tomorrow night I would be the new British welterweight champion. Roche didn't make eye contact with me once. He looked gun shy. So, how come then? He was 21-0. Let's go! Was he playing games with me? Maybe this was what he does; a bit of a games mistress. I put on my usual, over-the-top Blackpool front, which was igniting and irritating everyone. Good.

Coventry's Ryton Sports Centre was packed to bursting. I was rebranded, wearing my Superman shorts, boots and badge. I even had the Superman emblem shaved into my head, an idea styled after my idol Jorge Paez. It was time to go and I was ready for war. The Superman theme song filled the arena and I started my ring walk with cold, unblinking eyes. With adrenaline pumping through me, I was buzzing and focused.

The champ followed in soon after, accompanied by his traditional Irish music, in sharp contrast to mine. Now, considering he was fighting out of Yorkshire, I was surprised they weren't playing 'On Ilkley Moor bar t'at,' whatever that meant. Didn't matter, the crowd was up for it. The noise was deafening. The ref read the Riot Act to us. I went back to my corner to soak up some calm before the storm ahead. I looked at Roche, who was still avoiding eye contact. I gave Papa a kiss on the forehead, then ding. The bell went.

I raced to the centre of the ring, stopped, composed myself and set out my table plan. I started throwing jabs as Roche fired back, but I used footwork and speed to make him miss. 'Every miss is a wasted opportunity and a waste of energy,' Jackie always reminded me. 'Oops, too slow,' I said to him, every time he missed. I attacked his body, *pa-pa*, then sent a bullseye left to his jaw. He dropped down on one knee. Fuck me, I thought, the champ is on the floor already. He just managed to get up on the nine count. He held both gloves up for the ref, signalling he was good to carry on, but he looked shocked. It was the first time he'd been down in 22 fights.

I started to pick my shots with spot-on accuracy, raising the game, but he was covering up, killing time. My corner was yelling one clear instruction, 'Don't rush, take your time!' Twenty seconds later, the bell rang. I headed back to my corner, which was full of beaming faces.

'Good start, Scott. Pace yourself,' Jackie said, as I spat out water into the bucket.

Round two was not a lot different than round one. I was wrong-footing him, making him miss, catching him with more jabs. Blood was running from his mouth, which spurred me on, and my confidence was rising. I carried on, bashing him all over the ring until the bell rang again. Rounds three and four were much the same, and when we ended the fourth, Jackie told me that we were racing away with this. By his reckoning, I must be five points clear, if not six.

Two minutes into the fifth, Roche threw a right uppercut, which missed my chin button but caught me smack on the side of the temple. He followed up with a solid left hook. A couple of seconds later, my legs gave way under me. It's always a delayed reaction. Your body takes the blows, thinks about it for a second or two, then lets you know how it feels. Now I am taking the count. That's how quickly things change in this game ... *seven, eight, nine* ... but on nine, I was back on my feet. Roche knew he'd hurt me, so came in firing with both hands. I stayed out of his reach, as much as I could, firing the occasional cheeky jab. The bell rang. Thank Christ. I needed a breather. The faces in my corner looked more concerned now.

'You okay?' asked Jackie, cleaning me up.

'Yeah, bit dazed but okay.'

'Lead with that hammer jab. Knock on the door with that fucking jab and don't get sucked into his fight. You're better than that.'

In the next round, I got my senses back, hitting and moving at will. I landed almost every time he tried to make his way in and was boxing on the back foot. Papa banged on the canvas, telling me there was 30 seconds to go. I planted my feet and threw some heavy shots. Next thing, I felt a massive pain – a real thundering wobbler. He'd found a way into my right side. I sank like a stone in water to the canvas. Badly winded, I fought for air … *seven, eight, nine* … I stood up still fighting for air, trying to fill my lungs through my nose.

'What a brave performance Dixon is giving his fans,' I heard Adam Smith, the Sky commentator, say. I knew this was live on Sky Sports. I held up my gloves to show the ref I was okay, then we were back on. Two seconds later, the bell rang. I collapsed on to my stool, still totally fucked from the body shot. A lot of guys would've stayed down, knowing what was going to happen next. It's a long way back from a crippler like that.

'What are you doing, you stupid Scottish cunt?' snapped Jackie. 'What are you playing at? You're throwing it away. Stop trading. You are not a trader – okay?'

'My ribs are killing me. I think they're broken. And I can't feel my hands.'

'Fuck your ribs. They'll go numb as soon as you hear the bell,' Jackie said. Martin Bowers came over to me and pulled my shorts up to straighten them. He didn't look happy.

'We have an image to protect, son. It's shit or bust time now, so find a way to get to him,' Martin said.

Ding! Off we went again. Every breath I took felt like another body shot. There was something deeply fucked up inside me. A broken rib was probably pressing on a lung.

Martin's got a reputation to protect? I have a reputation to protect. I've got to nail him now – do or die. I started straight jabbing him, throwing the odd uppercut that got through. I was rocking him a bit, and his head was going up. He started stepping back, and I went after him.

We started trading. The wind doesn't know caution, even though Jackie had said mine should. But Jackie wasn't in the ring, I was. I wobbled Roche with a crunching left hook. He stumbled. Despite the noise, I could hear Adam Smith screaming into the microphone. That's how close he was to the ring. 'Dixon's going for the finish!'

I steamed in, alternating hands, but Roche was tough as old boots and was still firing back. He caught me on the temple again and my legs stiffened. He saw it. He pushed me on to the ropes, nailed me with a left hook then landed an uppercut that nearly sent me out of the ring. 'Now Dixon's in trouble!' Smith yelled.

I *was* in trouble and looking for a way to get off the ropes. The ref watched me closely and I was worried he might call it off. I was still fighting for every breath. My lungs felt full of broken glass. My grandfather and Jackie were both shouting. 'Fight back! Fight back! Come on!' The words hit home. From nowhere, I threw two quick hooks while Roche was in his corner. I hurt him. Through heavy and painfully fast breathing, I piled on the bombardment.

'Roche is on his last legs!' Smith shouted. Roche was bent double. My last uppercut should've put his lights out. It didn't. He was still here, but only just. He raised his head and took another three hammer punches on the chin. 'What an incredible fight!' Smith yelled as the bell went.

'You see, he doesn't like that. Look at him!' Jackie yelled. I still couldn't breathe but was feeling spiritually renewed. I checked out his corner. He looked as fucked as I felt. We were at it like a mongoose and cobra, and the fight could now go either way. I took round eight, for the most part, but it was hurting me to fight. My breathing was more laboured than before and I was probably bleeding internally. After the bell rang, my corner worked on my outside, but they couldn't fix my insides. No matter what I said, Jackie wasn't hearing it.

In the ninth, a few tasty jabs cut Roche right above his eye. Bingo! Now I had damage to focus on. But before I could start working it, Roche planted a big one into my left side. I went down again … *seven, eight, nine* … I got up. I couldn't feel my hands, so didn't know how well I was connecting. I couldn't feel my legs, either, so didn't know how I was standing. I was waiting for the final blow to end this. It couldn't be too much longer. I had nothing left. He came at me with both hands and I was on autopilot, defending myself any way I could. He threw a handful of shots that all hit my gloves.

I threw four left hooks, three hit his gloves, but one got him bang on the chin. Smith started yelling again. 'Now Roche is down! This must be the fight of the year!' I went to my corner … *seven, eight, nine* … He got up. I moved in for the kill, but the ref jumped between us, stopped the fight and sent me to a neutral corner while the ringside doctor checked Roche's eye. There was blood everywhere. I had a lot of his blood on me, even on my face. While I waited, I couldn't help but wonder if he had any diseases. Sometimes, strange thoughts come at very strange times.

The doctor spent a long time with Roche. He's got to stop this, right? Enough is enough. Even the crowd started calling for the fight to stop, which is something you rarely hear, but the doctor waved the fight on. I couldn't believe it, nor could my corner. Papa shook his head in disapproval and, by the sound of it, Smith agreed with him. 'This doesn't look right to me,' Smith said.

The only way to end this was to target his eye. Before long, it was wide open again and pouring so much blood he couldn't see out of it. The bell rang. In my corner, I watched his team frantically patch him up. 'There's only one round to go, Scott,' Jackie said. 'All you have to do is stay on your feet and you've won this. Nothing fancy, just do what you're best at.'

I danced cautiously, not getting too involved, but still working. I could see he knew he was beaten. He kept his distance, stayed out of trouble, risked nothing and counted the seconds to the bell. Ding! Ding! My hands went straight up. I was the new champion. I wanted to race over to the ref, but he was walking towards Roche. My heart stopped as he raised Roche's gloves. Even Roche looked shocked as his eyes glanced in my direction, then he shrugged sympathetic shoulders as if to say, 'That's how it goes.' My corner was all over the ref, but he was having none of it. The decision was final.

'Tonight, plain for all to see, Dixon was robbed, but that had to be the fight of the year!' Smith concluded while shaking his head. I was dazed and my corner quickly became gobsmacked speechless. At that moment, I wished John McEnroe had been ringside to scream at the ref. I couldn't believe his decision, either. The Sky panel gave me the fight by two rounds, while Dave Parris gave it to Roche by three. I don't know what fight Parris was watching but it sure wasn't this one. If nothing else, the match was voted the best fight of the year in 1999 by whoever rates those type of things. I did appreciate this later. But standing there on the blood-spattered canvas, while I felt my lungs wheeze, ribs creak, head pound and heart sink, I felt like a gladiator in the arena who'd been given the thumbs-down by a drunk Roman emperor. I wanted to throw the ref in the hotel cellar with Matilda and Geoffrey. Worse still, the night wasn't over.

Back in the locker room, I noticed blood in my urine and knew I needed patching up. Jackie and Papa insisted we go straight to Coventry General Hospital Accident and Emergency.

'You're in a bit of a mess,' the doctor said, frowning.

'You should see the other guy,' I replied.

'I think we already have,' he said, applying pressure to my ribcage. 'Does that hurt?'

'Yes.'

He listened to my breathing. 'Okay, let's get you x-rayed.'

I had four broken ribs, so I was strapped up tight like an Egyptian mummy. I had broken small bones in both hands, which also needed strapping up. I had a broken nose and needed five stitches above my right eye. God, what a way to make a living! I was physically and mentally broken. By the time the hospital had finished with me, it was too late to drive back to London. So, guess what? Another night staying at Coombe Abbey Hotel, but I was knackered enough to sleep.

In February 2000, four months after the Roche fight, I was working out on the bag at the Peacock Gym with fast left-right combinations. I'd been at it for a while when I clocked a guy in a brown leather jacket and blue jeans. He was watching my every move and staring more intensely than I liked. I hadn't seen him at the gym or anywhere else before. After I finished on the bag, I was wiping the sweat off my forehead when he came up to me.

'My name is Guy Ritchie, a movie director. Can I have a word?'

'Dunno. What about?'

'I'm looking for somebody who's around six foot tall with the right weight and reach. I just need a body, not a face. A body double, you know, for fight scenes. I think you may look the part.' I knew what a body double was.

'Oh yeah?'

'Yeah, other things, too. You're spot on for the chest and nipples,' he added without laughing. I gave him a sideways look and frowned. Nipples? What the fuck? One thing was sure, I wasn't dropping my boxer shorts.

'Okay, are you straight up or what?'

'Yeah, I need a body double for Brad Pitt.'

'Brad Pitt?' I thought about it for a second. 'Do I get to meet Jennifer Aniston, then?'

'Dunno, maybe,' he smiled. 'But you might get a film credit and a few grand.'

After I figured he was for real, we spoke a bit more. Guy was making a movie called *Diamonds*. Brad Pitt was the lead actor, playing a gypsy street fighter named Mickey One Punch. They needed someone for the fight scenes who matched Pitt's physique. Vinnie Jones was starring in the movie as well. I'd met Vinnie a couple of times before and it all sounded okay. Not my regular thing but I liked a bit of a change every now and then. 'Yeah, I could be on for this. You'll have to talk to my manager and trainer first, but I'm game for it if they are.'

After he spoke with Tony and Martin, Guy arranged for us to go to a location on Old Kent Road to meet his film producer, Matthew Vaughn. We drove to a Shell petrol station, where they were shooting some movie scenes. We hung around until they took a break. Martin was fidgety. No way was this his kind of scene. 'Bunch of fucking faggots,' he mumbled. 'What the fuck are we doing here?'

'Okay, 30 minutes, then back on set,' a man shouted. It was a bitterly cold day with ice on the forecourt and snow clouds gathering in the dark sky. I was dressed for the Arctic, wearing a big, thick-lined jacket, ski hat and scarf. My hands were stuffed into the wool-lined pockets.

'This is Matthew Vaughn,' Guy said. We shook hands and another guy joined us. He looked like a minder and resembled Mr T, a brick shithouse dripping in gold. 'Take your jacket off, Scott, so I can see your body again.' I started to unfasten my jacket and Martin stepped in like only Martin could.

'No fucking way. He's fighting in three weeks and ain't taking his fucking jacket off.'

'Okay, then he doesn't want the job,' Guy snapped, turning to walk away. Whether it was the cold, the Hollywood scene or both, Martin lost it.

'Go stick the fucking job up your arse, you cunt!'

Martin grabbed me, and we started to walk away. I wasn't happy. This could've been a good job with good pay. Martin stopped with a certain look in his narrowed, steel-grey eyes. I'd seen that look before.

'That cunt can't talk to us like that.' He walked back over to Guy and tapped him on the back. The minder jumped in between him and Ritchie.

'Get out of the fucking way,' Martin demanded while sliding his right hand inside his coat. I shot over to Martin, grabbed him and pulled him away.

'Just leave it, man. Forget it. It doesn't matter.'

Twenty minutes later, we got back to the gym. Martin was still seething, but Guy had phoned on the car ride back and I'd got the job. They were going to pay me £3,000 for a change of scene. You don't turn your nose up at that. Turned out, Brad Pitt was getting paid £12 million for the movie. But that was fair enough as I wasn't him.

Six weeks after my scrap against Sean Sullivan, which I won on points, we started filming the fight scenes in an abandoned warehouse in Islington. Its walls reeked of dank, putrid water and mould. Before that, we had regular sessions over two weeks in a cleaner place in Fulham. I taught Brad how to move, throw a jab, stop a jab and counterpunch on the back foot. We rehearsed, going over and over the routine, until Guy and Matthew gave us the nod.

The big guy who Brad fought in the movie's last scene was 'Big' Scott Welch from Brighton, the former British heavyweight champion. He fought Henry Akinwande in Nashville for the WBO title but was beaten on points, which was a bit of a letdown. He also stopped Joe Bugner, who'd come out of retirement. Scott was a tough guy and a self-made millionaire, who had also made a packet as a property developer. We got on, as boxers generally do. He worked with me and Brad at our sessions. Turned out, Brad was a quick learner and pretty good at this. He put a lot of effort into the sessions.

During filming, one thing I literally kept up my sleeve was my left hand. I'd recently fought the New Zealander Sean Sullivan for the Commonwealth welterweight title at York Hall in Bethnal Green, the home of British boxing and voted one of the world's most iconic venues. I'd busted my left hand during the fight. A tendon had snapped like an elastic band as I threw a left hand at Sullivan's head. I had to finish the fight virtually one-handed, and my left was my sledgehammer. But, I still ended up winning. After the fight, I underwent surgery on my hand and was still on painkillers.

It was still a momentous fight for me. There had only been three welterweight champions in Scottish boxing history: Tommy Milligan in 1920, Gary Jacobs in 1989 and now me. I'd beaten the world's seventh-best welterweight, as ranked by the WBA and the IBF. Fight night was also my girlfriend's birthday, and I'd bought her an engagement ring from an expensive place in Covent Garden. That night, I went down on one knee, like Prince Charming, and proposed to her.

'Do you want to get hitched?'

'No,' she replied flatly. 'Are you kidding me or what? I've got a flight to catch. See you later.' Cheeky cow. I had spent a fortune – and most of the purse money I was about to get – on that fucking diamond ring. It was time for a change of birds, but I'd keep her in the wings.

Even though the film was carefully choreographed, the fights were still physical. With a still-busted left hand, I had to bare-knuckle fight Big Scott Welch. Staged or not, we were both catching elbows and shots to the mid-section. As Brad's body double, I looked like a low-class gypsy from head to foot, with a pork pie hat, beard, trousers and braces, a scarf and Chelsea brogues. And because I had no hair, I wore a wig. People started calling me 'Pikey Dixon', but I'm no way remotely Irish. We did move around when I was younger, and Papa did have a caravan, but that was about it. I also got fake tattoos to match Brad's and he got fake tattoos to match mine. He even got my Glasgow Rangers tattoo that's on the left side of my chest.

So, even though my hand was fucked, I could fight the fights blindfolded, catching the punches, elbows and shoulders. I was in pain but got through it. Brad was good, too. Between training and playing a bare-knuckle fighter in his most recent film, *Fight Club*, everything turned out great, and critics praised the realistic fight scenes.

One night, I was out with Brad, Guy and Big Scott at The Rose pub on Fulham Road after rehearsing. We were having a couple of Guinness boilermakers and discussing being a 'wanted' man. Brad smiled and beckoned us to come closer to shut out eavesdroppers. There were plenty of them, all staring and smiling because he was in the pub.

'I was once the most wanted man in America,' he said quietly, then pausing for a second. 'I started seeing Robin Givens while she was divorcing Tyson.' Guy almost spat out his beer.

'Jesus, another pint, Brad?'

'It gets worse. One day, Mike turned up unexpectedly. He was banging on the door like a madman. Robin wouldn't open it, but I still hid in the closet.'

'That's a great story for the tabloids,' Big Scott said.

'Reckon not. That's just between us. He did see us later, though. He stopped by her house and we pulled up together in a car. He knew something was happening.'

'Are you nuts?' Guy asked. I was pretty shocked, too. I wouldn't want to see a pissed-off, jealous Tyson on the lawn. No way. I thought I'd change the subject.

'Is the film still going to be called *Diamonds*?' I asked.

'No, we're calling it *Snatch*. I wasn't crazy about it, but it stuck.'

'I like *Snatch*,' I said.

'Don't we all,' Guy said with a grin.

After a private screening, I went to a closed-door afterparty, a Hollywood tradition where alcohol flows and the who's who celebrate. I was still with my girlfriend, but marriage hadn't been mentioned since she rejected my proposal. We were at the very plush and swanky Waldorf Bar, just off Soho. Jennifer Aniston, who I did get to meet, was there, as well as Madonna, Claudia Schiffer, Jamie Foreman, who was the son of Brown Bread Fred, and a bunch of other *Hello Magazine* people.

Rumour had it that Freddy Foreman, otherwise known as Brown Bread Fred, had disposed of Jack the Hat for the Krays. Jamie Foreman had gone straight into acting, which was just as well. Camera lights flashed throughout the night, while the press clamoured for quotes to headline their stories about the screening. My girlfriend thought the event was dead cool. She hadn't experienced anything like it. I certainly hadn't either. Dressed to match any starlet there, she turned up wearing a little black dress and medium heels with her chestnut-coloured hair tied up. She got more than a few glances.

Surprisingly, there didn't seem to be a single snob at the party. We'd been worried that we might've felt a bit out of place. But we met and talked to everyone. My girlfriend blushed like a schoolgirl when she met Brad Pitt, who gave her a kiss on the cheek. Handsome charmer. Two could play at that game. I gave Jennifer Aniston *and* Claudia Schiffer, who were talking together, pecks on the cheek as we were leaving. One thing about Claudia: she is to-die-for beautiful in photographs and films, but in the flesh, face to face, she was even more stunning, if you can believe that.

The whole experience was a good diversion for me. It was a very different scene that got me out of my normal, rather grubby routine. I had mixed with people from a different world but very much doubted I'd be signing any autographs soon. My brush with Hollywood was interesting. That whole world seemed foreign to the life I knew, which was fine, but it was time to get back to some harsh realities. Movies and real life are quite different.

On 19 August, at the Fountain Leisure Centre in Brentford, I fought Steve Roberts for the WBF light-middleweight championship. I was the undefeated Commonwealth welterweight champion at the time, but I had stepped up a weight. It was my first fight at 11 stone. Steve had trained at the Peacock and I knew him pretty well. There was no grudge, so we showed mutual respect at the weigh-in. The fight was an opportunity for me to take another world title at a different weight. Whoever won this title was going somewhere. Steve, a southpaw who was also a switch-hitter, so pretty handy and unpredictable, was unbeaten in 21 fights. Although Jackie Bowers was optimistic about my chances, it was a real 50/50, 'who dares wins' kind of match. There was no doubt about that.

A couple of weeks before the fight, I'd spoken to my pal Paul Weir, the two-time WBO flyweight champion. He had been down at the Peacock on a publicity tour.

'Scott, I bumped into an old friend of yours, a girl named Stacy. She asked if I could pass her number on to you,' he said. I knew the Stacy he was talking about.

'Thanks, mate. You can definitely pass her number.'

Stacy was an old Hamilton Grammar School friend I hadn't seen for years. She was every bit as attractive as the current Miss Scotland – a proper glamour puss. I called her, and she was planning on visiting from Scotland to watch the fight. I booked her into the Britannia Hotel in the Docklands, where we were all staying. The prospect of seeing her raised my game. Now I wanted to put on a good performance against Steve in front of her.

When we got to the fight, we were all in high spirits. Stacy, my mum, Jackie, Martin, Papa and I were excited. The scene was like an east London derby, full of West Ham fans and ICF (Inter City Firm) football hooligans. Steve Roberts was also an ICF boy, so his fans were split into two groups. But, I had something he didn't have – an ICF tattoo. I was probably the only Scotsman who hung out with that lot, which was a bit strange maybe, since I was a staunch Rangers fan.

In the dressing room, I felt the beginnings of a headache coming on. With me, headaches come on pretty fast and I had suffered from them since I was in my mid-teens. Maybe a result of boxing, maybe not. Regardless, they're not the kind of headaches you can relieve with two Paracetamol pills. They're migraines – proper, full-on head bangers.

I usually took Migraleve, which were these little red and yellow tablets. When the headaches started, I took the red one to stop it, then the yellow one for maintenance. But I didn't have any with me and it was too late to get some. I started worrying a bit. Not only did these headaches hurt like hell, the migraines were optic, too. My head turned into a rave, with a pounding bassline and a light show. My vision quickly started flashing and blurring, and Jackie noticed me wincing.

'What the fuck's wrong with you, Scott?'

'I'm okay, I'm okay.'

'Well, there's *something* wrong. Why are you blinking?'

'I've got a migraine.'

'Fucking hell. Do you want me to pull this? I will.'

'No.'

We went through introductions and ding, the first round started. With migraines, first came the flash and second came the pain. Getting punched didn't help and this was a fight, not a game of golf. Migraine or not, I won the first round, then won the second with a combination of ability and sheer luck. I may have nicked the third by I whisker but in the fourth I took a couple of big shots to the head. I tried to cover up, but Steve got me with one straight on the temple. After the round, I sat on the stool gasping and blinking.

'What the fuck is wrong with you?' Jackie asked.

'Jackie, I've got the worst fucking migraine ever.'

'Okay, enough, I'm gonna pull you out.'

'No, I'm not going nowhere. I'm gonna see this through. Are we winning?'

'Yeah.'

By the ninth round, every little tap on the head felt 100 times worse than it should have. At one point, I got him on the ropes and was banging away, but a little six-inch stab of a punch caught me bang in the solar plexus and took all the steam and air out of me. Next thing I knew, I was on the deck … seven, eight … I was back on my feet. He caught me with a left hook, then switched to my body. Boom, I went down again.

Now I was on the floor proper. There were no three-knockdown rules with the WBF in those days, like the IBF and WBC. In the WBF, you could go on the floor endlessly until the referee stopped it. I went down four times and when I managed to beat the count again, he came at me with a barrage. I couldn't see … three o'clock, nine o'clock, 11 o'clock … I was punching into darkness. My eyes wouldn't open, my nose was broken, and I could feel blood dripping off my chin.

The referee grabbed me, looked me over and stopped the fight. Steve Roberts was the new world champion. The rest was a blur. I remember being in the dressing room and then, from what I was told, I collapsed unconscious. Next thing I can remember was being in Martin's Jeep, sitting in the back with Jackie.

'Stay awake, Scott. Stay awake!' Jackie yelled. 'Martin wouldn't wait for an ambulance, so we're taking you to hospital.'

Now, bear in mind that Martin and Jackie had lost little Bradley Stone in 1994. He died from a concussion and blood clot on the brain. There was a statue of Brad outside the Peacock. No way did they want to go through that again, ever. We arrived at the London Orbital Hospital, where I got checked over and had a brain scan. I can only remember half of it. I kept slipping in and out of consciousness.

About 7am the next day, I found myself in a hospital bed and started to think about how the fuck I had got there. Then, it came back to me slowly, piece by piece, like a jigsaw puzzle. Obviously, I'd lost the fight. Then another idea hit me. What about Stacy? She was in a hotel room in the Docklands and could definitely nurse me back to life. I pressed the help button and a red light came on. Eventually, a nurse came in.

'I'm leaving,' I said.

'No, you're not going anywhere.'

'I'm going. Take this stuff off me.' Reluctantly, she removed the drips from my arm. 'I'm getting the doctor. You can't possibly go.' She left the room and returned with a doctor as I was getting dressed.

'Mr Dixon, you cannot go. I cannot authorise this.'

'I'm going.'

I always had birds on the brain but never more than at that moment. I sat down near the hospital entrance about to phone for a taxi, but noticed a black cab parked outside with the driver reading a newspaper. I walked out and tapped on his window.

'Are you free?'

'Just having a break. Where to?'

'Docklands,' I said, climbing in the back.

The driver turned around and looked at me. 'Look mate, none of my business, but if you don't mind me saying so, you look like you should be in hospital. Are you okay?'

'Yes, thanks. Let's go, pal.'

For a bit, Stacy helped take my mind off the night before, but the fight had been a serious loss. It wasn't like the Carruth fight in Ireland, when I genuinely believed I hadn't been beaten. The referee must've had money on Carruth, but the loss against Steve was a real blow. Another stain on my clean sheet and it was hard to deal with at the time. That's when real, deep-rooted depression, which had come and gone in the past, really set in. Jackie had tried to cheer me up a bit. 'You have to taste defeat to appreciate success,' he said. That didn't help, but it was good to know he was still in my corner.

Problem was, I couldn't snap out of it. I went back to Scotland to Papa's place and told him and Gran that I needed to lie low, sleep and be left alone. They went along but their faces told me they were concerned. I knew Papa wanted to talk to me, but he was wise enough to wait until the time was right. I was right in the doldrums without a breath of wind. I was static. I couldn't get out of bed.

I felt similar to how I'd felt after the Carruth fight, but it was darker in every imaginable way. The curtains remained closed. I didn't want to see sunlight and didn't answer my phone. Usually the phone was always stuck to my ear, but not now. I switched it off, while something switched off in me as well.

Over the years, I sometimes had insane thoughts about driving my car flat-out into a brick wall or jumping off a bridge, but without any plan of when, how and where to do it. I had no idea where these thoughts came from. But they came in waves, then disappeared for a while. Things that usually interested me, like watching boxing videos, held no interest at all. I ate very little and nothing tasted of anything. I lost weight and someone else or something else was running the show. Satan? I couldn't look anyone in the eye. I couldn't hold a conversation without getting my words mixed up. And I found myself bursting into tears like a baby and waking up with my pillow all wet. After a while, Papa took me to see our family doctor.

'Clinical depression can be, and usually is, the result of a chemical imbalance in the brain,' the doctor said. 'It can be helped and indeed corrected with the right medication, though it can be a bit of trial and error.' He prescribed one thing, then another. Nothing seemed to make any difference, or maybe it did, but I'll never really know. One day, from some place, I just felt I should just hit a punch bag, which always made me feel better. Banging the hell out of something helped relieve stress and tension. I went back to the gym.

After my bout of depression, I become determined once again. The loss against Steve worked like a wake-up call. I needed to improve at what I did for a living. That simple realisation created a new, fresh and positive attitude within me. I had a fight coming up in Spain against an unbeaten fighter with a 10-1-0 record. In a sweltering temperature I wasn't used to, the fight would test my endurance and spirit. There was a lot riding on it, and I needed to know if I still had what it took. I also needed to test the durability of my will to win.

Round 6

A Bull in the Ring
18 May 2001

I was on an Iberia plane with Papa and Jackie Bowers on the way to Madrid. After a lot of hassle and contract disagreements, we finally struck a deal, but the fight wasn't going to be easy. I would be fighting a tough nut to crack, Rubén Varón, for the WBA interim light-middleweight championship. The fight was in Castilla La Mancha, Guadalajara, about an hour east of Madrid.

The venue was a bullring that would hold 12,000 very hostile Spaniards during the fight. They bought tickets to watch me get pulverised by their man. The most concerning thing about Varón was the way he looked. He looked like an actor or fashion model, a good-looking guy who didn't appear to have ever been hit.

Papa had always told me, 'Don't worry about the guys with flat noses and bashed-up faces. Watch out for the good-looking ones. They don't get hit much *and* they're special.'

Varón must've been the best-looking guy in boxing. I had to see what I could do about that.

He was on a winning streak, but I was a seasoned pro with 29 fights under my belt. I was also trying to come back after two successive KO losses to Steve Roberts and Anthony Farnell. For me, it was probably now or never. But I was fighting at light-middleweight now and my new weight was causing me a few problems. Stepping up a division usually required some physical and mental adjustments. Also, I only had four days' notice before the fight.

On the flight, the seatbelt sign came on with an accompanying 'ping'. The cabin crew sat down and strapped in – not a good sign. Suddenly, we were in turbulence and being pummelled and buffeted around. A locker dropped open and two luggage bags dropped down, landing on the passengers sitting in front of me. They were stunned and one of them was bleeding from the face. Normally the crew sorted this type of thing out in a flash, but nobody was moving. They stayed strapped in like they must've known something we didn't.

Was this an omen? A foretelling of things to come? A few people had tried to talk me out of this fight but it was now-or-never time for me, and I needed to restore my status or jack it in.

'Are you alright, Scott?' Papa asked.

'Yeah, why?'

'Your face looks like parchment, your hands are shaking, and you've spilled tea all over your trousers.'

The tense atmosphere of the flight carried over to the weigh-in. Nothing usually fazed my grandfather but having 12 Spanish security guards eyeballing us, following us everywhere, and yelling at us in Spanish was starting to get to us all. Varón and I both weighed in at 11 stone exactly, so we were even on that score. But I had a longer reach by three inches, which doesn't sound like much, but it is.

The changing rooms were typically for matadors, toreadors and picadors. The walls were lined with photographs and paintings of men who obviously had a lot of status around here, as well as the bulls that raged and roared and snorted no more. Bull fighting had always struck me as a very bloody form of one-sided entertainment, where the animals had no chance – except on the very rare occasions when the bull got the upper hand and gored the living daylights out of someone.

The event was scheduled for 2am, a clear tactic of the Spanish designed to create an advantage for Varón, as if a bullring with 12,000 Spaniards behind him wasn't enough. Me, Papa (proud as punch waving his Union Jack) and Jackie made our way to the ring through the very hostile crowd. Two Spaniards threw punches at me, but I blocked them. I jumped into the ring and yelled at the crowd. 'Come on, come on!' I waved my fists, egging them on.

Varón's theme music started up and he marched towards me while 12,000 voices chanted, 'Rubén! Rubén! Rubén!' There was no top on the bullring, so at least some of the racket went up and out of the arena into the humid night. Varon had a big Basque following and there was a lot of money riding on him that night, so if he lost, we'd need protection. As soon as he was in the ring, I ran over to him sharp. 'You're getting it tonight, Varón! Just you see! Jabbing for Jesus, Varón!' The seconds before the first bell always got my heart pumping but never more than at that moment.

Papa leaned over the ropes and called me over. 'I know you're up for this, but do you want to do it?' I put my arm around his neck and kissed him on the forehead.

'Bit late for that, isn't it?' I smiled. 'In for a penny, in for a pounding!'

The bell rang. The only way out now was to kill the bull.

During the first minute, we were both cagey, sizing each other up. Varón was a solid fighter. He had a good jab and a fierce left hook, but my pinpoint jabs were getting through. Then, I caught him with a cracking straight left and felt the impact inside my glove. This guy had never leaked blood in a fight but now blood was pouring out of his nose. I could tell the sight of blood made him very uncomfortable and it was like a red flag to the bullring crowd. They went mental in that hot-blooded, Mediterranean way. Then the bell ended the first round.

'Just keep doing what you're doing, Scott. He doesn't know how to handle you. He wasn't expecting that. You drew first blood on pretty boy and he doesn't like it. Aim for his nose,' said Jackie.

He came out in the second round like a man on fire. Now he was boxing like a Mexican, moving and swaying from side to side real fast. He landed some tasty body shots. I was feeling them but showing nothing. He worked on my body, but I was firing machine-gun jabs in return. He hit me with a low blow, a long way below the belt. I fell to my knees and then looked up to see the ref giving me a count … five, six, seven. I got up on the eight count, put my hands up to show the ref I was okay, and the bell went. I walked over to my corner and collapsed on the chair.

'Fucking Spanish cheats. That low shot was on purpose. The ref chose not to see it,' I said, still breathing heavily.

'There's only one way to win this,' Jackie said. 'Lower the standards. Fight the fight he's given us.'

The fight was not going my way. He was focusing his assault on my body, knowing I was still hurting from the blow that put me on my knees. He had another edge on me as well. He'd been training for this fight for months whereas I'd been pulled in as a substitute. I'd only had four days' notice and the only training I'd done was keeping my general fitness, certainly not the kind of fine-tuning required for a top fight like this.

Varón knew I was hurt and kept targeting my body. I tucked up, covered up and stopped most of his shots, but the odd one was getting past my defences. I threw straight jabs every time I spotted an opening but then shipped another thumping low blow, much worse than the last one. My bollocks felt as though they were stuffed into my groin. I looked to the ref to take action but instead was given another count … six, seven, eight. I managed to get up before the nine count. The only thing to do now was to slug it out, toe to toe, and play his game. If he wanted to fight dirty, he would get it.

The bell went, so I got a breather. It was hot as hell fighting in that bullring.

'You're going to have to knock him out, Scott. This is a set-up,' said Papa.

'Yes, it is,' I replied, sucking in air. 'I've felt it.'

'You've gotta put out fire with fire,' he added.

Just before the bell, Jackie tapped me. 'Don't let this fucker get away with this shit. Nail him any which way. Just win.'

As soon as round four started, I caught him off guard with a straight right that rocked him. Now it was payback time. I threw a low blow. He hit the deck and rolled over. You'd think I'd scored a cup final goal in my corner. Jackie was jumping up and down, while the crowd booed, screamed and hurled abuse, programmes and cigarette lighters. I'd hit their matador in the bollocks. Instantly, the ref deducted a point from me. Of course, he also gave Varón more time than I'd been given to get himself back together, but now I knew I had a chance. I could smell it. He looked shocked and unsure, like in the first round. It's always there in the eyes.

I was getting on top of him again when he struck another low blow. Jesus fucking wept! This time, the ref took a point off him, which I thought was strange. I figured the ref's palms had been well greased enough to overlook Varón's cheating completely. The bell sounded to end the fourth. I walked to my corner with my hands in the air. It would've been two middle fingers if my gloves had been off – a gesture that crossed language barriers. Jackie gave me some experienced words of wisdom.

'Throw a jab, miss and put your head in fast, so it looks like an accident, then nut him but apologise to the ref. This *is* a dirty fight. I don't like it, but you need to finish him any way you can.'

The bell for the fifth sounded and I did exactly what Jackie said. I threw a jab, missed intentionally, then headbutted him. The 12,000 Spaniards roared their disapproval. He was cut, bleeding and dazed. Varón probably thought I wouldn't fight dirty but he had started it. Somehow the ref hadn't seen it, but the crowd certainly had. The headbutt took all the confidence out of Varón. I threw a hammer-blow left to his chin, a sweet right uppercut, then another left and a right jab – *pa-pa* – all bang on the money in three or four seconds. He fell back against the ropes dazed and wobbling. He was nearly gone, and I had time on my side.

I flicked the switch and went into overdrive with my foot flat down. He sent nothing back and I nailed him without letting up. There must've been another two minutes to go before the bell. It was no longer a fight and he was taking way too much. This was the danger point when people can die. Although I decided to ease off a fraction, I was also there to win. I tried to nail him with one massive right when the ref jumped in and stopped the fight. If I had kept up the barrage, I might have hospitalised him.

I dropped to my knees in sheer relief, while the crowd noise quickly subsided to near silence. For a split second, you could've heard a pin drop. Then the loss sank into the crowd. Their matador had been gouged by a fucking Scot and the crowd started to realise it. But the night wasn't over yet. We were on foreign soil with very different rules of engagement. Their boy had been a cert bet and most of the crowd had lost a ton of money. Tonight, they'd lost their faith in their champion as well. In the humid Spanish night, you could feel the tension starting to boil.

My cornermen jumped in to congratulate me. Papa draped the Union Jack around my shoulders and jumped up into the air. I was worried he was going to dance a little jig around the ring. 'Dixon, you're back!' Jackie shouted. 'What a finish against these fuckers! What a stitch-up. We're not coming here ever again. You can quote me.'

'Where's the belt, then?' Jackie asked a Spanish official, who pretended not to understand and walked away. As a rule of thumb, the belt would usually be handed to us now. These jokers. They had their own rules about boxing and they had their own rules about belts. 'Fucking dago cunts!' Jackie said.

I had seen someone put the belt underneath the ring at the end of the fight, but nobody had seen this – of course. They just threw their arms up, protesting their innocence. The wankers weren't going to hand it over. Anyway, the main thing was I'd won the fight. The belts were always great for photos but that's about all. Still, after you won a title match, you'd wear it, swanking off to the crowd for a brief moment in time. It was a good feeling, but the belt wasn't a big deal.

The *real* battle now was to get from the ring to our changing room without getting shot. For 12,000 demoralised and probably poorer Spaniards, they needed someone to blame, and we were in the crosshairs. More police than I'd ever seen at a fight surrounded us and ushered us in a cordoned, military-quick fashion out of there. We got back to the Arena Hotel, where we were staying. Our bags were waiting in the lobby, along with the hotel manager, who was wearing the face of a lost sheep.

'No charge, so please go now,' said the concierge in broken English, who was standing in front of his hotel manager like a bodyguard. 'It's not safe here for you or for us. We have received a warning of a death threat if we provide you with any accommodation.' His hands were shaking, so I figured he was telling the truth.

We got a taxi and left in a rush, while police bikes and more police cars escorted us.

'Right, fuck this for a nightmare. Let's just get out of this fucking country now,' said Jackie.

'Now or tomorrow?' Papa asked.

'Yesterday would've suited me fine,' responded Jackie in a huff. 'We ain't doing this again with these fucking twisted, cheating Spaniards. Good thing my boys aren't here, but … you did a cracking job, Scott. I nearly jumped in to give you a hand. I was going to deck the fucking ref. You were in the snake pit!'

We went to the airport and managed to get on a flight to London, but it meant a long wait.

'We could get a flight to Paris and take it from there,' I suggested.

'Fuck off,' said Jackie. 'We're not going around the houses. We're not going to France. We're going straight home.'

In spite of all the commotion, and now ignoring any physical damage I might have received, I was on cloud nine. I needed that win badly. I got £15,000 for the fight. But more importantly, I had regained Jackie's respect and Papa was proud of me. That meant everything. A victory celebration would have to wait until we had planted our feet firmly back on English soil.

Round 7

A Bloody Battle in Manchester

July 2001

'It's another Tequila sunrise ...' That's how I felt and that's what I heard playing somewhere in the distance. I was lying face-down by the pool with Fiona, a jewellery designer for the celebs. I'd been examining her jewels these past few days and we were nursing the mother and father of hangovers. I'd first met Fiona at Hamilton Grammar School when we were kids. We were in the same class together, but she never paid much attention to me in those days. It was party time in Ibiza and the island was in full swing 24/7. I had decided to take Ibiza on at its own crazy game, and the island was definitely winning. We were both knackered. I felt like I had been embalmed but Fiona was still able to walk in a reasonably straight line.

'I need two hairs from two dogs. Can you be a babe and go get us two large vodkas and coke? I can hardly move,' I asked her.

'Oh, okay.'

'No ice,' I shouted after her.

I watched Fiona waddle over to the pool bar thinking she was definitely one of the hottest things on two legs, and everyone else around the pool was watching her thinking the same. The only thing between her and complete nudity was the smallest bikini I had ever seen on a woman. Her bikini bottom was no bigger than a Moshe Dayan black eye patch held together by two black strings, and the bikini top wasn't much bigger. Just enough fabric to cover oyster pearls. In Ibiza, even in a smart hotel, you could probably get away with wearing nothing at all. People over there rarely had their clothes on for very long. My mobile rang but the number was private. As a rule, I never answered calls unless I knew who was on the other end. But for some reason, on that occasion, I did.

'Hello?' I answered, trying to disguise a voice that had been out all night.

'Is that you, Scott?' The Cockney voice sounded familiar but in my state of total disrepair, with steam hammers banging in my head and bells ringing, I couldn't immediately place it.

'Yes, this is Scott. Who's this?'

'It's Frank Warren, son. What are you doing next Saturday night?'

'I don't know, Frank.' I figured it was a social call. Maybe Frank wanted to invite me to dinner or a party or something.

I couldn't think straight. I wanted to hurl my fucking mobile into the swimming pool.

'Do you want to fight Jamie Moore on Saturday? His opponent pulled out because of an injury, or so they say. I know it's real short notice but there's £7,000 cash in your pocket if you're up for it.'

I didn't have to think about it. I needed the £7,000. I'd blown a stack of money in Ibiza already. The island was a total wallet-emptier. It happened without you even noticing what was going on. One minute, you had a stash of notes and next minute, you were cleaned out and nearly skint.

'Yes, okay. Count me in, Frank. You'd better let me have the details.'

'Fantastic. I thought you'd agree, so I already booked you and your corner into the Radisson. The fight is at the Velodrome in Manchester. You're on the Ricky Hatton bill, and it'll be for the WBU international light-middleweight championship. I hope you're fit, boy, so you can give this kid a bit of a fight. I expect nothing less. I'll confirm the hotel and the fight. Glad we're on and see you soon.' He hung up.

His tone left me with an impression. Frank just wanted me to turn up and take on this up-and-coming prospect as a fall guy. I'd read a bit about Jamie Moore in boxing magazines and the papers, but I didn't know how he fought, what his style was, nothing. I didn't even know he was a southpaw until I checked him out, but I did know he was undefeated. That was always a bit of a mountain to climb. The undefeated always thought they were undefeatable. But nothing lasts forever, especially in boxing. One day, the canvas would come up to meet you.

Fiona came back clutching two large glasses stuffed full of ice. She bent over as three guys stood up without leaving their sun loungers. These holiday destinations always filled your drinks with ice like you're an idiot. I reached out to take a glass and my hand was shaking like a leaf in a breeze. Jesus Christ. How the hell was I going to get in shape to fight anyone in less than a week? I couldn't even swat a fly. It was Sunday and I was a proper mess. As I began to digest the phone conversation with Frank, the prospect of Saturday already started looming.

'Are you alright, Scott?'

'No. Not really.'

'You look like you should be in hospital. Good thing you're not fighting any time soon.'

'Yeah,' I smiled.

'Christ, I'm so done-in from last night. I don't want to do anything. No sex, nothing,' she whispered playfully.

'I hate to say this, but I agree.'

We were leaving Ibiza at 6am the next day anyway, so there was no point hurrying to leave the island today. It was our last night and we had tickets for Space, one of the world's most famous nightclubs. I figured we might as well make an all-nighter of it, then go straight to the airport with bags packed. We caught the flight by the skin of our teeth, still blasted out of our skulls. We fell asleep before the plane took off and woke up when we landed. As soon as I got home,

I switched on my answering machine and heard one very pissed-off Jackie Bowers. 'Where the fuck are you? Taking fights when you haven't trained? Meet me at the Radisson in Manchester at 10am on Tuesday. Don't be late!'

I hadn't yet told Jackie or Papa about the fight. What was I thinking? I should've assumed Frank would've contacted the gym about it. I couldn't think straight. I needed a week of sleep with nobody else in my bed for once. I set my alarm clock for 6.30am. My train left from Glasgow the next morning but wouldn't get into Manchester until 10.30am. Unfortunately, just like Papa, Jackie had a thing about being on time. He was going to go mad if I was even a second late, but I didn't really have a choice. I walked into the Radisson and Jackie was sitting in the lobby looking at the floor. He spotted me and met me in the middle of the lobby.

'Sorry I'm a bit late.'

'Where the fuck you been? If Frank hadn't called me, I wouldn't have even known we had a fight, would I? You think it doesn't matter? It fucking well does matter, you twat.' He began to calm down a bit.

'Okay, Scott. The fight is in five days and this boy is tasty. All the betting is already on him and by the looks of you, I can see why. I want you to check in, *please* take a shower, then get into your training gear. Be back down here by midday.' I was about to answer but Jackie wasn't having it. 'Not a second later. Is that clear? Good.'

Had I done the right thing here? If Jackie had done his homework on this boy, and really did fancy him, I was in deep shit. Jackie knew fighters and a severe beating and terminal embarrassment could be heading my way. Still, £7,000 was £7,000 and I had left all my money in Ibiza. I went downstairs bang on midday and Jackie introduced me to Mickey, who owned a gym nearby. We had some hard-graft, non-stop work to do between now and the fight.

It was a gorgeous, hot day in Manchester and as we walked to Mickey's car, I noticed north of England birds were fit. In England, there were definitely more women in the summer. We drove about 20 minutes to a housing estate, a wee bit posher than in Glasgow, but only just. I even noticed that some gardens still had flowers. But the boxing gym was like a scene out of *Shameless*. It was packed out and reeked of sweat, urine and shit-stinking toilets. It was the kind of gym most would run a mile from, but it beckoned me like an old friend. I walked over to the old-fashioned boxing ring in the centre of the big, cold room. I climbed in with Jackie, who threw me a skipping rope.

'This is your lifeline, Scott. Get warmed up. We have to blow these cobwebs – and God only knows what else – off you. Go to work.' One of my natural skills was skipping rope. I knew the moves, how to switch and speed up instantly without ever getting the rope caught. Within ten minutes, I started to attract a crowd. The more they watched me, the more I showed off. I've always liked being on stage. One hour later, I started to feel Ibiza ooze out of me one drop of sweat at a time.

By Friday, everyone at the gym said they'd come and support me at the fight. They were all top-dollar boys in my book and were lucky to have a guy like Mickey running their gym. Jackie always knew the right people. There wasn't anyone else who could've fixed me in a week, including Papa, who had arrived midweek to help with the training sessions.

The first time I had the chance to look Jamie Moore in the eyes and suss him out was at the weigh-in. 'He's just a boy, Jackie,' I said.

'Yeah, a boy who hasn't lost yet. He isn't called "The Fighter's Fighter" for nothing. Just focus and try to wind him up, so we can see what he's made of.'

I looked in Moore's direction. Ricky Hatton was giving him advice about me. Moore looked like a typical Manchester skinhead and was loud with it, already mouthing off. I knew how to deal with lippy fighters and always did the same thing to push them. I needed to know where the fighter's ledge was. In the ring, it may make it easier for me to push them off it. I smiled and blew him a kiss. That always got them going. We stood there, toe to toe and face to face, for the photographers. Moore cursed like he only knew four-letter words in that snappy, irritating Mancunian accent. He kept telling me I was going down in the second round.

'Who are you, you little cunt? I chop up little boys like you 'til there ain't nothing left,' I said. He put his face right up against mine until our skin touched. The security men jumped in to separate us. For me, it was all fun and games. He was all mouth and trousers. Jackie seemed pleased with the outcome. The whole spectacle was just part of it.

'Good job, Scott,' Jackie said quietly in my ear. 'He has a temper and no control over it. It's a young fighter's curse.' Just to check that hypothesis out, I blew him another kiss and he came running at me. Security pulled him off again. Yup, young and impetuous. 'Let's get out of here. I hate these northern cunts,' Jackie said. 'They think they're something and rarely have anything to back it up.'

Next day, we arrived at the Velodrome in Sport City, Manchester and I was shown to a big room where all the undercard fighters were getting changed. Screw this. It was all part of their game plan to undermine me, but I wasn't falling for it. Jackie went nuts and tried to get hold of Frank Warren without any luck. No surprise. Nobody was going to be accommodating or reasonable. That was obvious.

'These fuckers are trying to stitch us up,' Jackie said. 'Doesn't matter. Just focus on me and do what I tell you. Let's get ready to fuck these northern twats and show 'em what's what. Remember Spain? Against the odds, we did it. You're still the champ. Get a fix on that and don't let it go.'

Jackie shouted out combinations while I warmed up by hammering the pads. There was only one more fight, which was in progress, then it was my turn. I was feeling a little apprehensive and angry, but altogether fired up. From the dressing room, I could hear the 18,000-strong crowd chanting, 'There's only one Ricky Hatton! There's only one Ricky Hatton!' As one of Hatton's protégés, Jamie Moore had the backing of the entire stadium. I probably had around a dozen supporters, mostly from the gym or in my corner.

All week in the papers, TV and radio, Hatton had been asking all of Manchester to get behind his big prospect. The pundits played along, describing Moore as the new Manchester sensation who was destined for the top. Of course, according to the talking heads, it would take a miracle for the Scotsman to pull it off, especially in front of a Manchester crowd. I started wondering if they were right. What was I thinking? I didn't train enough. Was £7,000 worth a beating and the embarrassment? Fortunately, there was a loud knock on the door to steady my nerves. 'You're on Scott, shake a leg,' said a voice without a face.

I entered the arena and a capacity crowd of morons screamed for Jamie Moore while tossing abuse at me. There was a lot of unbridled electricity in there, all fizzing and popping. The racket was like a thunderstorm right bang overhead, when a flash of lightning and a blast of ear-numbing thunder happen simultaneously. We were in for an explosion. This was a re-run of Spain all right.

It seemed strange to be champion but still the underdog (and getting paid so little), but that's how it went sometimes. I needed a mental stimulant. I'd read about a mountaineer who used to carry an orange in his backpack. Although the orange added to the weight, he carried it with the idea of eating it on the mountain top, spurring him to greater heights. I needed a tangential idea like that.

I promised myself that after *I won* this fight, I'd go back to Ibiza for a few days for a well-deserved holiday. Better than an orange.

In the ring, I started showboating to the crowd just to see how loud the boos could get, then Jamie swaggered in. He jumped into the ring and you'd have thought he'd just scored the winner in a World Cup Final. These Manchester blokes were seriously off their rockers. They didn't want a win. They wanted blood. The ref called us together and chatted the usual dos and don'ts, clean fight, what I say goes. I looked through Jamie's eyes, right into the back of his head, to show him I meant business. I wasn't just another step on the ladder he was climbing. The bell went.

He came at me, firing on all cylinders, with both hands ablaze. His strategy must've been to get the fight over and done with fast, sending the Scot back to Scotland. Like a freight train, Moore had penetrating ammunition and an arsenal of seemingly endless firepower. Who the fuck was this kid? Age was on his side, too. All I had going for me was experience and staying power, but I wasn't in shape for this – at least not big-match, fully charged battery in shape for this. But it was my fault. Too much Ibiza, too much of everything.

I was taking lefts and rights, then uppercuts followed by some well-targeted body shots. His workrate was astonishing and punishing. It seemed to take forever for the bell to ring, like the round was five minutes long, not three. I walked to my corner, with blood streaming from my nose and mouth. I sank down on the stool and looked up at Jackie. Fuck this for a game of soldiers. Only £7,000? I've earned that already, not that the crowd would agree. They wanted me dead and carried on a stretcher by four men wearing kilts. The judges must've had him streets ahead already. I looked outclassed. It was hard to hear what Jackie was saying above the racket, but I picked out a few words.

'I told you not to underestimate him. He's dangerous, on a roll, and thinks he can't lose. So far, you're not doing anything to change his mind. Keep him off, use your left. Change his mind!' Papa was nodding in agreement. He didn't look happy about the way the fight was going. I knew both Jackie and Papa were pissed off that I'd accepted the fight without checking with them first. There was being ready and not being ready for a fight. I was not ready, physical or mentally.

Ding! In round two, I was dealt the same barrage as in the first round. This runaway express train didn't stop coming. It was as if Moore had been computer-programmed to punch at an abnormal speed. It just didn't seem real. Then, and I'm not sure if I imagined it or heard Jackie yelling at me, a plan popped into my head:

> If you can survive a few more rounds, he may punch himself out. He's overdoing it and thinks he can drop you early, so keep your distance. Look for your chances and make every one count. Use your left like a sledgehammer. Like a brick wall, keep him off you.

Whether Jackie had said this or not, it seemed like a good strategy for now.

The bell sounded in the nick of time again. I walked slowly to my corner. Last week, I was getting ballooned on a beach in Ibiza and now I was taking a hammering in front of 18,000 Brits who wanted my blood. I should not have agreed to this, especially for £7,000. Should've been £70,000. Neither consequence of my newfound strategy was very appealing. This fight was either going to be a punishing slog – allowing Moore to pummel me until he tired – or very short with my lights out. Walking back to my corner, a very convincing half of me was saying just to call it a day.

'Do you want to go on with this, son? You don't have to,' Jackie said with eyes of concern he rarely showed. There was something about Jackie's eyes and the idea that I had disappointed him and Papa that sparked something deep inside of me. Too right I wanted to go on. I'd started this, so I needed to finish it. I never walked away. Jackie patched me up and the dreaded bell rang for round three. No turning back now.

I quickly took a barrage of more bad medicine. Just before the end of the round, he got me with a terrific body punch that knocked the wind clean out of both me and my sails. I went down and stayed there until the count reached eight. I nearly stayed down but my fighting instinct wouldn't let me. Jackie always said 'ride the bike' when things got really tough, so I tucked up, grabbed him and hung on until the bell rang. I couldn't do nine more rounds of this.

I was on the stool with my head down. I might as well have been on the floor. Jackie cleaned me up with the skilled hands of a master and the ref came over to check me out. 'Fight him back now. He's starting to blow,' Jackie said with his mouth in my ear. I didn't know if Jackie had seen something that made the slightest sense, but the words recharged my spirit nonetheless. I sent a message to my inner reserves and the reply came to my rescue. 'Every man has his moment,' Papa used to say. With Papa in my corner tonight, it was now time to find out if this was my moment. Ding!

During round four, I stood my ground better than in the previous rounds. While blocking almost everything he threw at me, I returned hard, solid jabs that connected – ones your knuckles feel through your gloves. Sweat flew off his face. Then I launched a few one-two combos that hit their marks. I saw something, in a split second, that Jackie must've seen earlier: Moore was blowing and couldn't hide it. His mouth was gasping for air and his spit, punch and speed weren't the same.

Moore was suddenly being cagier and more thoughtful, slowing it down and taking breathers, altogether regrouping his resources. It could've been a cute ploy to bring me in, so I had to find out by turning up the heat. I had no idea how much I had left in the tank, but neither did he. My eyes weren't giving anything away. It was also encouraging to hear his corner shouting. 'Back off now, tuck up, slow it down. Take less,' they yelled with an air of surprise.

'With about 20 seconds to go in the fourth, I caught him with a full-on left uppercut, quickly followed by a straight right bang on the chin. This was the moment of truth. Was his chin rock or glass? I backed it up fast with a two-fisted onslaught. Some missed, some glanced and some connected.

He was on the ropes but still upright. The bell saved him, but I had delivered some serious damage, both physically and mentally. I don't think he knew what had hit him. His corner, by the looks of them all, didn't know either. I jogged back to my corner and waved my right glove to infuriate the crowd.

'I told you, son! He's finished,' Jackie said. 'Doesn't have anything left. Go back and do the same thing. Don't stop until you've knocked him over.' For the first time all night, I welcomed the sound of the bell like a good friend who'd come to call. If I wanted this fight, it was now or never. I needed to be fast, direct, furious and especially focused to expect the unexpected. I didn't know what kind of reserves he had. He could also throw one and get lucky. It only takes one punch.

I went at him, ramming my long jab into his face, then shot a right straight-bang into the centre of his chest. I was tiring and on my last legs, but he was exhausted. He'd given 80 per cent of all he had way too fast and was now hitting the wall. I'd been there and done that when I was younger. It happened. Suddenly, it hit me that I wanted to win this more than he did. All the signs were there. I'd seen it many times before. It's usually the turning point when you tighten the screw.

Halfway through the round, I hit him with a decent one-two that sent him backwards to the ropes. During the longest half minute of my life, I rained down left and right hooks, body shots and uppercuts. I threw 25 shots in 30 seconds. The last shot was a blow to the back of his head. The golden boy was on his way to the canvas. You don't throw a shot like that intentionally but once you've thrown it, you can't pull it back. I watched Moore try to scrape his body off the canvas while listening to the count … *seven, eight, nine – out*!

Same as Spain. Fifth-round win. Maybe five was my lucky number. Now winning was one thing but concern for your opponent was always another. So, I watched until I knew he was okay. Celebration could wait. Jamie got up and the crowd gave him a standing ovation. I went over and put my arms around him. 'You're good, pal,' I said. 'You nearly had me.' I was pronounced the new light-middleweight champion and the crowd, whilst disappointed, applauded me. Papa beamed me a smile and gave me a thumbs-up.

Headlined in the *Daily Record* as 'Dixon Had Moore on the Night', Ewing Grahame wrote:

> Hamilton's Scott Dixon became Scotland's latest 'champion' when he stopped local hero Jamie Moore to win the vacant WBU International light-middleweight title at the Velodrome in Manchester.
>
> Moore had won all 12 of his previous contests but Dixon made it unlucky 13 for the Englishman by knocking him out in the fifth round. It was an astonishing turnaround for the former Commonwealth welterweight champ, who looked certain to suffer a sixth defeat (from 31 bouts) earlier in the fight.
>
> Moore started superbly, landing half a dozen punches for every one he took. He won the first three rounds, the last by a two-point margin after he dropped

Dixon with a left hook. The Scot displayed courage to bounce back, hurting Moore with a barrage of punches towards the end of the fourth.

That set up a memorable finale. Moore was short of stamina and was felled by a six-punch combination. Moore failed to beat referee Dave Parris's count and the belt was Dixon's.

Dixon said: 'I only had a week's notice for this fight but it was enough. He hit me with some real hard shots in the third but I thank God because he gets me through these fights.'

Round 8

The End of the Line

2005

I met Pamela at the Palace Nightclub in Hamilton. It had been months since I'd been released from hospital after the attack on my life by McMillan and his accomplices. Although I was cagier and more alert to my surroundings, I needed to start going out and living life again. Tonight, Pamela was covering for a friend who worked behind the bar and waited tables, but I'd clocked her a few days ago at the club. She was wearing black jeans, a dark-green silk shirt and black Gucci flats. When we finally had the chance to talk properly, I didn't catch her last name because of the noise but she came back to my place and, as simple as that, we started dating. After being together for a few weeks, she made it clear that she was serious about the relationship. 'I'd like you to come home and meet my mum and dad,' she said. That's when you either cut and run or stick around and see what happens.

'No problem. What's your dad's name?'

'Billy.'

It was a bright Sunday morning full of promise. We drove to a house that looked like the Ponderosa and parked outside a three-car garage. Taking in the house like an estate agent, my mind was calculating and putting a value on everything I saw. A few acres of garden were fenced with CIA alarm systems and there were dog kennels in the distance. Pamela opened the front door and we walked on to a polished parquet floor in a hall that was several times bigger than the whole of my apartment.

A black grand piano was centre stage with the lid propped open yawning. There were two white marble statues that flanked the staircase. They looked like the real McCoy and worth a fair bit, but I'm no expert and I had stopped calculating. Gold curtains framed three huge leaded-light windows. Maybe Billy's a concert pianist?

Pamela introduced her mum, Katherine, and I could see the likeness. She had the same sparkling emerald-green eyes. We shook hands and I gave her a kiss on the cheek, which I hoped wasn't too presumptuous. She smiled.

'Oh, meet my dad,' Pamela said as Billy walked in to join us.

My reaction was immediate as I clapped eyes on him. *Fucking hell.* I was almost worried I had said it aloud.

I'd never once met 'Bilko' in the flesh but I'd seen his face in the *News of the World* once or twice. Now I was sleeping with his only daughter. This could go any fucking which way. I took a deep breath and smiled.

'How you doing, pal?' he asked in a squeaky Glasgow voice.

The word 'pal' meant fuck all. It was like an American saying 'Have a nice day.' I'd know how I was doing if I left today on both feet. Jesus, I made a mental note to always get someone's last name in future.

'Okay, thanks. You?'

He didn't reply.

Katherine laid on a fantastic lunch like royalty was coming for a meal. We sat down in an expansive dining room at a table that could seat 12. Hanging on the longest wall were huge, framed oil paintings of the Highlands and Highland cattle. Below the paintings was a massive marble fireplace with huge oriental-looking vases flanking it.

Lunch was quite formal, and we chatted about nothing in particular. I was attentive and polite but mainly silent. I was on my best behaviour, whatever that was. I felt this was like an interview without any questions being asked. I was trying to hold my knife and fork properly like my mum had always insisted growing up. The seared-to-perfection roast beef and seasonal vegetables were excellent. The meal was paired with a magnum of French red wine. Judging by the label, the wine was probably something I hardly ever touched but I genuinely liked the juice.

Katherine did most of the talking, mainly about how she'd always wanted to go to Egypt and see the pyramids, but Billy was always happier in Spain on the 'Costa del Crime' with his pals who'd gone there to live for one reason or another. Throughout the meal, Billy seemed to have one eye on me.

I could see that. He was checking me out, sizing me up like a fighter at a weigh-in. But, if I failed his eye test, it probably wouldn't be 'Goodbye *pal*, see you soon'; it would be 'Goodnight, Scott Dixon.' Billy was a dangerous guy who nobody messed with. All the rumours about him weren't hearsay, they were facts. If he wanted to, he could just lift the phone and I wouldn't make it back to Hamilton.

After lunch, Billy asked the girls to leave us. Pamela shot me a little smile and a wink as they headed off towards the kitchen to make coffee. I tried not to look at Billy's glass eye – no easy feat. I'd heard that once, during a street fight, he'd been hit with a big shaft pole on the side of his head. The pole hit him so hard that his eye popped out, then someone stepped on it in the mayhem.

'You want coffee?' he asked.

'Not if you're not having it,' I replied, not really sure how to reply. Billy was quiet for a second and looked me over.

'Okay, I've heard what you're about, Scott. Word travels a bit. From what I hear, you can handle yourself and don't get bothered easily. Would you like to go for a drive after lunch?'

'Sure.' You didn't say no to an invitation from Billy.

We hadn't driven too far from the house when Billy stopped the car. 'Open the glove box, Scott.' I pressed the button and the lid fell open. Inside, there was a piece and a box of shells. I didn't want my prints on it, so I weighed the gun with my eyes.

'Yours if you want it.' This was all a bit sudden and definitely not what I imagined when I accepted the invitation to meet Pamela's parents. I didn't know if the gun was a gift, a threat or a bit of both. I snapped the compartment lid shut.

'Thanks Billy, I know where to find it.'

'Maybe you and me can work together and see how it goes, yeah?' he suggested.

'Yeah, why not?' And that's what we did.

In the beginning, we worked together as a two-man unit. We moved quantities of coke and made good money, but Billy always wanted more – more product, more profit. I knew this fella who we called Moiffy as kids. Moiffy was as talented and knowledgeable as any college-educated industrial chemist. He called it working his magic wand, which wasn't a bad way to describe it. Moiffy could make four kilos mysteriously appear from only two kilos – like magic.

We employed Moiffy straight away and within no time the money started pouring in. That wasn't an issue. Our problem was more self-inflicted. It wasn't that our train *started* having trouble staying on the tracks; we pretty much derailed pulling out of the station. One day, Billy asked if I wanted to move into his house and live with him, Katherine and Pamela as a family. At the time, I didn't know the extent of Billy's past drug problem.

Shortly after moving in, Pamela and I were sitting in the bedroom talking. She told me that Billy had been addicted to heroin and crack cocaine six years previous. The problem eventually became serious enough that Katherine had to give him an ultimatum. So, to keep the marriage, Billy got clean and had been since. Of course, I knew otherwise but didn't dare say anything about it to Pamela. I changed the subject.

'Wanna go out tonight?'

'Sure, but not to a club. Can we go out for dinner?'

'Okay, I'll fix it.' I rang up and booked a table at the City Café on Finnieston Quay. It was a place Katherine had mentioned more than once.

'Where are we going?' Pamela asked, pulling up her tights while removing every last crease in the fabric.

'Surprise. I hope you like it.'

'I like surprises. Do you?' she asked, stepping into a slinky silk dress. She checked herself out in the mirror while she gently adjusted her shoulder straps.

'Depends. You look great. Those colours suit you.'

'Thanks. Can you zip me up?'

'I'd rather unzip you.'

'One thing about tonight, though.'

'What?'

'I said I didn't want to go to a club but what I really mean is, I don't want any trouble tonight. Can we please not meet up with your friends?'

'God's honour. You'll have my undivided attention.'

We sat down at a table on a balcony overlooking the Clyde River with a good view of Squinty Bridge.

'Mum likes to come here with her friends,' she said, her eyes searching the menu.

'That's why I chose it. Katherine has very good taste.'

'We should do this more often. It gives us a chance to catch our breath.' Pamela picked up her glass of wine, looked across the restaurant and raised a hint of a frown.

'Best behaviour?' she asked, her eyes still looking over my shoulder.

'I gave you my word.'

After a few seconds, a man I hadn't seen before was now standing by our table.

'Pam,' he smiled.

'Robbie.'

'How are you?'

'This is Scott. He's ... err ... my fiancée.'

'Yeah?' Robbie said, stealing a glance at Pamela's left hand.

'Yes. We're out having a quiet celebration. Otherwise, I'd ask you to join us.'

'No, I'll leave you two lovebirds in peace,' he said with a hint of sarcasm. I waited until Robbie had left the table before speaking.

'Fiancée?'

'If you want,' she said. After a few seconds, she added: 'And another thing ...'

'Go on, surprise me,' I said, draining my wine glass.

'I'm pregnant.' I coughed and spluttered. Pamela rose from her chair and slapped me hard on my back.

'I thought you had an extra glow about you," I said, still catching my breath.

'Who knows? Maybe it's twins.'

'Jesus!'

The waiter came over to our table. 'Can I get you anything, sir? Are you ready to order?'

'Another bottle of the same and a double Scotch – no ice, no water,' I said. 'We'll order food when you bring the drinks, thanks. Any recommendations?'

'Everything, sir. What would your lady like is the *real* question?' he answered, shooting Pamela a smug half-smile. She laughed as he walked away.

'Ponce.'

'No, he's charming,' she said. 'He has manners.'

'Get on with you. Does your mum know? Or Billy? Does Billy know?'

'If you want, you can ask dad if you can marry me but for right now, I'll only break the baby news to mum.'

'Okay,' I said, letting out a long exhale. 'I have to buy you a ring.' Through dinner, I tried to look enthusiastic and happy. But, with Billy, I was already in deep water. Now, with this, I was sinking faster while the water was getting deeper.

Not long ago, I'd met a bird named Laura at a party during a night out with the lads. We had pitched up late and I'd spotted this stylishly dressed woman wearing a short, figure-hugging red dress. Red's my colour. She was a very tasty blue-eyed blonde and body-tuned like she worked out in a gym or went swimming every day. She was standing alone looking at her watch. Either she was waiting for someone or thinking about leaving. I made my move.

'Hello, who are you then?'

'Laura.' No way was I going to make the same mistake again about not getting a surname.

'That's my favourite name. Laura who?'

Federico Peltretti

Jim Murray (7 December 1969–15 October 1995) before the fatal bout with Drew Docherty
Mirrorpix

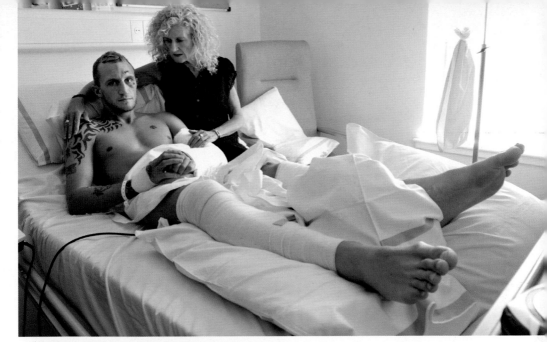

Scott with his
mum, recovering
in hospital after
the 2004 attack
outside his home
in Hamilton
Mirrorpix

Scott celebrating his 1998 win over boxer Chris Saunders at Thistle Hotel in Glasgow
Mirrorpix

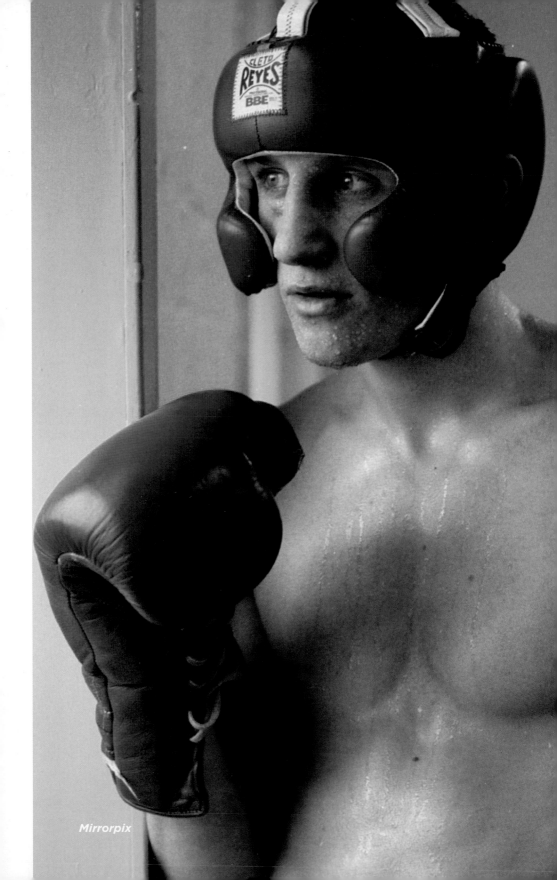

Big Alex Morrison outside the Barrowlands in Glasgow **Mirrorpix**

Matthew Marsden (centre) with Scott and gym co-owner Martin Bowers at the Peacock Gym **Mirrorpix**

Scott skipping rope at Peacock **Mirrorpix**

Guy Ritchie, Brad Pitt and Matthew Vaughan at London's Snatch *screening* **Getty**

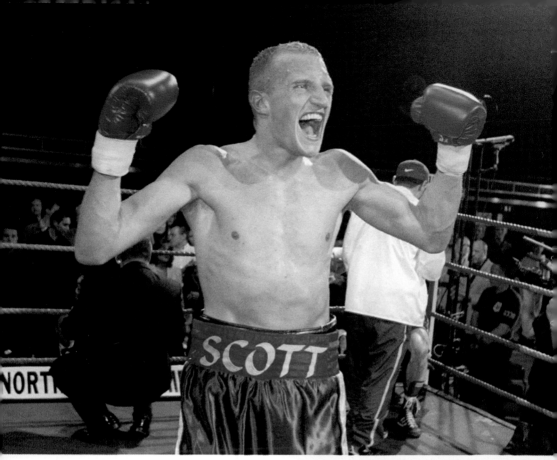

Scott celebrates his win over Charlie Kane at the Motherwell Civic Centre in 2000
Mirrorpix

Federico Peltretti

'Laura Raphael.'

'Ah, like the painter. You know, Raphael was also the name of the archangel who said, "It is God who heals." I learned about both of them at school once upon a time.'

It wasn't the best chat-up I had ever put together. She gave me an odd look, then her eyes glanced at the door.

'So, there's no way you're single looking the way you do,' I quickly added.

'On and off,' she smiled. 'Why do you ask?'

'It's against my nature to invade on someone else's territory,' I lied.

'Oh, is that so? Then you'd be one of the few guys in history who'd actually care.' She laughed and wrinkled her nose. Nose-wrinkling got me every time. It's one-up with a dimple. Give me both and I'm anybody's.

'Can I get you a drink?'

'Oh, go on then.'

One of the guys I'd gone to the party with came over, but I nodded him away. He got the message. I was on 'mission possible, mission likely'. When I gave a woman my full attention, they got just that. Over the years, I'd trained my eyes not to wander around the room looking at other birds. As it often was, the encounter with Laura was pretty natural and instantly gratifying: mutual attraction, a few drinks – then far too many drinks – then bed at her place.

A few weeks later, though, I made the simple encounter more complicated. I was still sneaking off and seeing Laura behind Pamela's back at almost every available opportunity.

The idea of getting engaged to Pamela was one thing. You could always get unengaged. But the idea of a baby was a different matter altogether. Jesus. Why do so many women have babies?

I decided to go with the flow for the time being. I should've come clean with Pamela then and there at the restaurant – faced the music before she found out – but I didn't. And women always do find out, one way or another, sooner or later. They have a sixth sense about it. They can smell it.

When we got back to the house, Katherine and Billy were still up and sitting in the kitchen on opposite sides of the table. It was clear our arrival had interrupted a conversation. There was a cool mood hanging in the silence, and I noticed that Katherine's hands were clenched tight into fists.

'Have a good time?' asked Katherine in a quiet voice. She looked like she'd been crying.

'You okay, Mum?' asked Pamela.

'Ah, yes and no. I was telling your dad that things need to change. The police were here tonight on some pretext. Your dad sent them packing,' she said, looking straight at me.

As if Pamela thought this was a perfectly normal time to proceed with our plan.

She nudged me in the ribs and whispered, 'Go on.' I took a deep breath and then, considering what was really on my mind, spoke a little reluctantly.

'Not sure if this is the right time, Billy, but would you be okay with us getting engaged?' Billy just looked at me, showing neither surprise, delight nor annoyance.

'Scott, come with me.' I followed Billy out of the kitchen, down the corridor and into the drawing room. 'Stay here. I'll be back in a minute.'

I sat down on a sofa and stared at an oil painting of a prize bull that was hanging above the fireplace. I heard the cellar door being unlocked and the sound of Billy's footsteps descending into silence. Only Billy ever went down there. When he came back into the drawing room, he was holding a shoe box. He tipped out the contents on to the coffee table and waved me over.

'If you two are serious about it, and you know she can be a handful, then you'd better have one of these. Cast your eyes over these baubles. There might be something in here to suit the occasion and tickle her fancy. Are you sure about this, Scott? Or, have you been railroaded? You know what women can be like.'

'Hmm,' I nodded positively, though my mind was swimming as I looked over the contents of the box. There were gold rings, necklaces, brooches, earrings and watches – Patek Philippe, Rolex and Cartier. I singled out one ring with a big rock in it. As I picked it up, I felt even worse.

'Is this okay, Billy?' I asked, whilst eyeing a gold Rolex that must've been worth at least ten grand.

'Course it is. Don't want you buying nothing from some fucking flashy jeweller in Glasgow who'll rip you off.'

'Ta Billy.'

'If it doesn't fit, I've got a man in town who'll sort it. Just say the word.'

Katherine came into the room with Pamela in tow. Pamela looked down at the diamond ring I was holding and smiled. I looked past her at the door. Should I leg it? It was now or never.

'Pamela's got something to tell you, Billy,' said Katherine.

'I'm pregnant, Dad.'

'Just as well you got engaged then,' said Billy as he left the room.

After he left, Katherine looked at me with her tired, soulful eyes. 'Might be a good time to slow down and take stock. You have two people to think about now, Scott. But I imagine nothing much will change.' She looked like she'd had quite enough to deal with for one night.

'Yes, Kat.' Katherine kissed Pamela, then me, and left the room.

A few weeks later, things were deteriorating on all fronts. Nobody wanted to do business with us. We were becoming maniacal in our dealings and home life was just as bad. Pamela may have had her mum's looks, but she did not possess her mum's sense of loyalty, though her actions were probably more retaliation than anything. I didn't blame her. She'd caught wind about Laura and reacted. She had started seeing her ex-boyfriend, a Glasgow criminal named David Murphy.

She was still pregnant with my child – or maybe it was his child. I had no idea. Words are often full of lies. Laura must've pushed her over the edge and out of the house. I knew I had started it, along with all the rot that had followed. Trust had gone out of the window and it wasn't ever coming back.

She disappeared for three days and Billy stayed up most of those nights pacing the house waiting for her to return. At about 3am one morning, I was woken by screaming from downstairs. I could hear every word.

'Get out and don't come back!'

'Don't you worry, Dad, I won't.'

'I know where I stand with Scott, but I have no fucking idea where I stand with you!' he yelled.

'You have no idea what you are saying, as usual. Talk to him about what he's been doing. Ask him about Laura,' she said in a monotone. I heard the front door slam then the car spew gravel.

A few minutes after the fight, Billy opened my bedroom door. 'I have no idea what that meant. You're better off without her, son. Take my word for it. We've a busy day tomorrow, so you had better get some sleep.' There was no way I was going to be able to sleep. What a fucking mess.

We'd done business with this Murphy, who Pamela was seeing again, in the past. One day, he tried to turn us over for a few grand, saying that a delivery had never turned up. We knew it had. After that incident, Billy had it in for him. I never dared tell Billy the whole story about Laura, but I was sure he knew about it anyway. I prayed that Pamela had kept silent about it. Billy's beliefs about marriage and fidelity were deep-rooted. He didn't understand why people should ever mess about. 'Messing about with other women breaks hearts and ruins lives. It's a very costly pastime,' he once said to me.

We were told that Murphy was seen driving into a Beefeater restaurant on the outskirts of Glasgow. We got loaded and went to the restaurant completely out of our minds. Billy was armed with two guns that he had named Ronnie and Reggie. Once we found a spot to park, he pulled them out of the glove box and stuffed them into his coat pockets. 'Billy, forget the guns, for Christ's sake.' I managed to get the guns off him and put them under the passenger seat.

Billy just looked at me, got out of the car, went to the boot and pulled out two machetes. Under the car park lights, the machetes were shining like newly polished silver. He walked back up to the passenger door. 'I'm going to chop him up.'

'Billy,' I started in, but then just left it alone. I knew it was a waste of breath. We walked up to the restaurant. Through the window, I could see Murphy with two guys who had their backs to us.

'He's on the table with two fellas at the far right by the wall,' I said quietly.

'Only come in if it turns nasty,' Billy said and walked hurriedly towards the front doors of the restaurant.

I watched as Billy threw open the doors of the quiet family restaurant and marched over to the wrong table. 'Shit, one-eyed git,' I said to myself. But before I could do anything, one of his machetes came down clean on a random diner's arm. People turned and stared in disbelief until the reality of the situation sank in. I ran into the restaurant. 'Billy, stop! Stop!' The place turned into total chaos. Mothers and fathers picked up their kids and ran for their lives.

Murphy also made a run for it, but Billy saw him and kicked a chair in his way to slow him down. Right as Murphy started to stumble on the chair, Billy hit him with a machete bang in the centre of his back. While Murphy stood upright from the pain, I hit him with a fierce right hand that sent him to the ground. Murphy's two mates ran to his aid and Billy stabbed one of them in the chest. I grabbed Billy, rushed him out of the door to the car and drove the hell out of there, just in the nick of time. A mile down the road, police cars with ambulances in tow raced past us towards the restaurant. The sirens cut the air like razors then faded. 'Billy, we've got to lie low. Only a miracle can save us from being identified. What about getting out of the country? Spain, maybe?'

'Maybe.'

Everything business-wise continued to spiral down. Moiffy, the chemist, fucked up in a massive way and landed us in deep shit. We owed a ton of dough. He'd gotten right out of his fucking pram and I'd sensed the day would be coming sooner or later. It turned out to be sooner. Moiffy had been banging on about an American-made pharmaceutical that the Jamaicans called 'magic' – an intriguing notion for a self-proclaimed magician. The drug not only mimicked cocaine but when it was cut with pure cocaine, the cut product would still register near 100 per cent. The stuff was already in London, so Billy called the supplier and we hit the road. The plan was to buy 20 kilos from a geezer in Bethnal Green.

When we arrived at the destination, the lights in the house were out.

'You sure this is the right place?' I asked Billy.

'Fuck knows.'

'Is this a stitch-up?'

'Let's find out,' he said whilst handing me a 9mm automatic. We walked to the door and rang the bell. We waited for a minute then rang the bell again. I heard a noise from inside the house, then a voice spoke.

'Yeah?' asked a gruff voice.

'This is Billy.' A light came on from the hallway, visible through that glass pane in the front door.

'Billy who?'

'Billy Glasgow.' A man with two-foot-long dreadlocks opened the door and stood in the doorway. He was wearing shades and holding a 9mm automatic.

'You got the money?'

'Yeah,' Billy replied.

'Stay there.' He closed the door and locked it. A minute or two later, he returned.

'Come in.'

'Where's the stuff?' asked Billy.

'It's all here.'

We loaded the tubs of so-called magic into the car and paid him. Two other guys appeared from nowhere and watched us while the money was being slowly counted. All of it was Queen's head up. He stopped counting and had to start again. Thick bastard. 'Okay,' he said after counting twice. Billy removed his hand from his coat and we left in a hurry.

Driving back to Glasgow, we had no idea what was in the boot of the car. It could've been flour, sugar or any fucking thing. It was shit or bust time. 'I hate these fucking immigrants,' said Billy. 'Did you see what that cunt was holding?'

'What?'

'It looked like a fake gun but I wasn't going to take the chance. We could have blown them away and left with this shit. Fuck me, this stuff better work.' Now that we had the magic, all Moiffy had to do was wave his wand over it and the cash would come in like falling rain.

Billy and I were sitting in the kitchen reading the papers when I got a call from Moiffy. 'Come to the allotment. Got a wee bit of a problem,' he said. We pitched up and made our way to an old shed in the middle of the allotment area that was neatly divided up into large and small rows. Some of the allotments were full of tomatoes, cabbages and sprouts; others were filled with roses and dahlias; and a few sprouted nothing but weeds and thistles.

I banged on Moiffy's shed door. He peered out at us through a tiny window with a cracked glass pane and let us in. On a battered picnic table with folding metal legs, a dozen plastic bags filled with orange gunge were bubbling like a light-coloured tomato soup over a gas flame.

'A wee bit of a problem, you said?' I asked.

'What the fuck? A *wee* bit of a problem, you said!' Billy yelled like a maniac. 'Do you have any fucking idea what's at stake?' Billy bent over and looked into the tubs of magic with their lids off. 'Are you fucking blind? What does that fucking say on the label, you cunt?'

'Oh,' Moiffy said, looking closely at a label clearly marked: DO NOT LEAVE EXPOSED TO AIR.

The air had gotten to the magic while Moiffy mixed it 50/50 with the kilos of pure. We hadn't yet settled the payment for the kilos, so now we were in debt and in the shit. Billy looked at Moiffy and spoke in a monotone that was subduing his rage. 'Go outside and dig a fucking grave in this allotment of yours. Then come back in and sort this out or you're in it. If you and Scott didn't go back a way, you'd be fucking dead already.'

Moiffy had been smoking crack all day. I could see it in his eyes. Now his life was on the line. He knew that Billy meant what he said. Moiffy only had one chance, and limited time, to sort out the shambolic mess. Billy wanted to kill him, that was obvious, but killing Moiffy wasn't going to solve our problem – the ton of debt we were facing.

'We could try slowly drying it out,' Moiffy suggested.

'Fuck you!' Billy shouted.

We loaded the bags of orange shit, bags of pure and the tubs of magic into the boot of Billy's car, then we drove like the wind to Comet in Glasgow to buy three dehumidifiers. We took it all to Billy's house. He had a massive store cupboard with a double electric socket inside. Moiffy put the bags into the cupboard, switched on two dehumidifiers and closed the door.

'Now we pray,' said Moiffy.

'Now you pray, you mean,' snapped Billy. 'How long do we leave it in there?'

'Twelve hours should do it,' said Moiffy. 'I'll check it every four.'

After 12 hours, the orange shit was a little dryer but still fizzing. We chucked in another kilo of pure to soak up the moisture, but it made no difference. We might as well have slung £35,000 out of the car window. The stuff was probably dynamite, but it looked like the Jolly Orange Giant had got hold of it, so it was untradeable except to the blind. That left Billy owing a ton of money.

If all of this wasn't bad enough, Moiffy and I noticed that tiny corners had been cut off the cocaine bags, and the weight was down. Naturally, Billy then noticed and accused us of ripping him off.

'It was fucking you, because it wasn't me,' I said to Moiffy.

'I thought it was you, so I turned a blind eye,' he replied.

It wasn't the wisest thing to have said within Billy's earshot, but Moiffy always spoke first and thought afterwards.

'Sorry Billy.'

'I'm watching you and your lips very closely from now on, you cunt,' Billy replied.

Obviously, Billy was skimming it off and not saying anything. He was a serious closet coke-sniffer in complete denial or delusion. It was hard to tell which one. People call coke a recreational drug, but bollocks to that. We were all snorting the profits and our slippery white slope was getting steeper. Billy's paranoia and megalomania had become increasingly worse, and his lethal side was showing its ugly face more than usual. He was already a fucking maniac, but coke was a fuel to Billy's fire.

Next day at 9am, we got in the car. He opened a plastic CD cover with fat, pop-star lines of coke neatly laid out.

'Let's sharpen up to kick off the day,' he said.

'Bit early for me, Billy. Later on.'

'Suit yourself.' Billy snorted two lines then sniffed the intake loudly three times.

'That's better. Let's go make a killing.' We were driving down Lansdowne Road on Glasgow's outskirts when Billy tapped me on the arm.

'See that guy over there?'

'Yeah.'

'Run him over.'

'Wha?'

'Do it,' he snapped. I mounted the kerb but he turned, saw us and ran off.

'What was that about?'

'You missed him. He owes me money and he's late.'

If you handed Billy money, and it wasn't all stacked Queen's head up, he'd likely stab you. Along with his other mental and behavioural issues, Billy also had a serious obsessive-compulsive disorder. He wouldn't step on cracks between pavement stones and if he spat, he always spat three times. Needless to say, being late with a payment didn't register with how Billy's brain worked. Things were starting to heat up. Serious crime squad started coming to Billy's house, and we were getting stopped regular by the Old Bill. While we were dealing drugs, we also started our own brand of boxing products. More than anything, the endeavour was kind of a piss-take with two middle fingers up to everyone. Bad Boys Boxing Products sold gloves, shorts, t-shirts, tracksuits and kitbags. The name was on both sides of Billy's Mitsubishi Shogun to draw attention to the brand, but all it did was attract the police. We'd get pulled up almost every day, which fucked off Billy massive. One day, when Billy wasn't with me, I was driving my black BMW convertible down Bridge Street wearing all the Bad Boys gear when I got overtaken by a police car and waved over.

'Right, bad boy, out the motor,' said a young cop eyeballing me.

'When you find nothing, I want a fucking apology.'

It was time to teach them a lesson. DS Edgerton, who we called Edgy, helped operate drug squad surveillance. He worked 'undercover', which was a laugh, because he stood out like dog's balls in his chinos and blazer. Cops seem to have only one pair of shoes, the regulation matt-black, Mr Plod sort.

I was in Rakes Bar on High Street chatting with Edgy and kidding him about his shoes. He'd had a few and was a bit wobbly, slurring his words. I fuelled him with four shots of neat vodka and he was talking real rubbish. I had him right where I wanted him.

'Me and the lads are going to a party in Bothwell. Do you wanna come along?'

He meandered over to my car, nearly fell over and we took off. When we arrived, I had to wake him up.

'Evening all, wakey wakey, ello ello!' I helped him out of the car and into a terraced house that was jam-packed with people.

We kept Edgy well oiled. He stayed on his feet but barely. His eyes were rolling, and he could barely string two words together, let alone say 'the Leith police dismisseth us' or walk.

'Where am I?' he mumbled as his eyes closed. He soon crashed on to the sofa with his mouth wide open. Three of us unzipped our trousers, pulled out our cocks, placed one on his shoulder, another on his head and one about two inches away from his open mouth. We took about ten photographs whilst pissing ourselves laughing.

Since we continued to be stopped, harassed and searched as a matter of routine, I finally put my plan into action. I called Edgy and asked if he wanted to meet me at the house. Always trying to extract information, I knew he'd agree. He took every opportunity to hang out. I got him some coffee then I handed him a brown envelope trying not to smile. He may have thought it was full of folding.

'Anyone else here?'

'No.' Edgy ripped it open, pulled out half a dozen photographs, flicked through them and his face dropped.

'Fuck me.'

'Precisely.' He tore them up and threw the pieces at me.

'Plenty more where that came from. Should I send these to *The Sun*? Pin 'em up on the station's notice board? If you don't lay off me and Billy, I will.'

'I won't forget this,' he said. 'I thought we had an understanding.'

'We do now.'

While I was able to steady the police harassment problem, Billy was another story. The only time he wasn't off his rocker was when he was at home, but Katherine knew the wheels had come off his wagon. I'd been wondering how long Katherine would put up with old Billy, then one day I found out.

'Scott, can you come upstairs?' she shouted down the staircase just as I was heading for the door one day. She was sitting in her bedroom doing her nails by the window that overlooked the manicured lawns. Two doves were sitting in a tree watching her. She looked at me without smiling.

'What wrong, Kat?'

'I know Billy's using again. His eyes give it away. I've lived with this before and can't do it again. I can't put up with it much longer.' She sighed and shook her head.

'I'm not sure if me talking to him would be any use,' I said.

'You need to change your life, Scott. Go to Australia, Los Angeles, Vegas, anywhere. Go and train fighters or get into something else. Carry on like this, and you'll end up in prison or killed.'

'I'll do my best to help, Katherine, I promise.' She looked straight through me, then closed her eyes and blew out a breath of despair. Her words struck home but I deflected them. For now, I was in too deep for a life-change.

Although he entertained his demons, Billy was as crafty as he was crazy. He worked in an old people's home two hours a day and wouldn't miss it for anything. He genuinely loved old people and always banged on about his grans. He appreciated their experience and the stories they'd tell. The old people at the home loved Billy in turn. For some praying for death, he was their only visitor. One day, his affinity for old people offered us an opportunity.

'Scott, we need a safe house to stash and I think I know just the place – the old folk's home.'

'Oh yeah?' I couldn't help but laugh a bit. It was a brilliant idea but strange to think about.

'Yeah. Most of the old folks don't haven't the foggiest idea who they are or where they are. I don't see the harm.' The next day, we went to the home. I carried a holdall and Billy brought flowers and a box of chocolates. There was nobody about. Billy tapped on the door of Room 6 and we walked in.

'Hello, Mary, darling. Happy birthday,' Billy said, sitting down in a wooden chair next to the bed.

'Is it? Thanks, Billy. Nobody told me.'

'These are for you.' He handed her the flowers and chocolates. 'And this is my pal, Scott. He's come to mend your cupboard.'

'That's kind, Billy.'

I opened the cupboard door, took out clean sheets, an old handbag and a few curios, then unscrewed the backboard, placed four kilos against the wall and screwed the backboard into place.

'They'll think you've got a fancy man,' said Billy, smiling at me.

'Go on with you, Billy,' she giggled while Billy took her hand.

'See you tomorrow, darling.' We walked out of the building, still without seeing anyone about.

'It's no place to end up, is it?' I said.

'No. You'll never find me in a place like that.'

We also rented a warehouse in an old, disused industrial area. When we arrived, the guy who owned it was waiting for us. He unlocked and opened the steel doors, used another key to unlock a sliding metal-barred door, like in a prison, then walked into the darkness. He switched on the lights. A second later, six fluorescent tubes flickered then illuminated the warehouse with bright light.

'It used to be a toy warehouse and I've still got boxes of 'em in here. I can't shift 'em on my own. I'm not supposed to lift anything,' he said, leaning on his walking stick for support.

'You can leave them here. They'll be safe with us,' said Billy.

'Thank you, boys. That's very kind.' Billy handed him six months' rent in advance and his eyes lit up.

'Oh, that's crackin'. Let me know if you want to rent it for longer.' He handed us the keys, limped slowly to his van and drove away. I ripped the strips of gaffer tape off one of the boxes and opened it.

'Hey, Billy, get a load of this.' I opened another box. Billy stared at the contents and smiled. 'This is like Christmas, Billy. Look at this stuff. Teddy bears, Muppets, the Sesame Street gang, Miss Piggy, Kermit the Frog ...'

'Right, got an idea. Get the holdall from the car and let's get cracking.' We spent the rest of the day stuffing bags of coke into the puppets then resealed the boxes.

A week later, I was at a party in Hamilton. I was as wired as a searchlight and near overdosing because of too much coke, but wanted more. I drove to the warehouse, unlocked the steel door, slid back the prison bars and walked in with a flashlight. The light was jumping around over the walls and cardboard boxes, and I couldn't keep it still. I grabbed my right wrist with my left hand and tried to steady it. I ripped open one of the boxes, pulled out Miss Piggy, and stuffed my hand up her skirt with my fingers searching for the bag of coke.

'Taking my stash and interfering with my bird?' asked a gruff-voiced Glaswegian.

I shone the shaking torch in the direction of the voice. Kermit the Frog had risen up from the box and was staring at me. I was hallucinating.

We were on a collision course and it was only a matter of time before everything collapsed like falling scaffolding. I knew Katherine was at the end of her tether. I was still staying in the bedroom Pamela and I shared before she left. One night, I heard a heated argument downstairs. I went to see what all the commotion was about. I opened the kitchen door, where the racket was coming from, and walked in on a very serious domestic situation. Katherine stood with her arms folded and eyes blazing. She wasn't budging until her opponent backed off for good.

'No, Billy, I don't want anything to do with you any more. I want a divorce. It's final and been coming for a long time.' I saw the sadness in Billy's one, real eye. He worshipped the ground Katherine stood on. He picked up a coffee cup, threw it against the kitchen tiles above the oven, and stormed out of the house, slamming the door behind him so hard the house shook.

'Well, fuck you!' he yelled from outside. I turned to Katherine with a plea in my eyes.

'Katherine, please don't do this. You can see how unstable Billy is. He'll do something stupid. I'm begging you. Tell him you were hacked off and didn't mean it. Give him a chance.' My words must have lit a fire.

'You've no idea, Scott!' she yelled. 'We've done this before! Before, he wouldn't see the doctor, go into hospital, rehab, nothing. I had bars installed in the windows of the upstairs back bedroom to lock him in. He'd scream blue murder and hammer on the door, then go quiet. I was afraid he was just waiting for me to come in.

'I was terrified out of my wits to ever open the door, so I called three strong men, who you know, to protect me while I took him food and water and cleaned up his puke and shit. I hired an asylum nurse to check his heart and everything. Once you've done all that, you've spent all there is to give, no matter how much you love them. I'm drained beyond empty, I can't take any more. This is not me. You may move from bitch to bitch like a wayward lost dog, but I'm true to my vows, Scott, and I'm choked to death with all this.'

She burst into tears. Nothing could've stopped Katherine's outpouring until she'd let it all flood out. She'd thrown in the towel and walked away in her mind already, if not long ago. The iceberg was bottom side up. I sat down beside her with Billy on my mind. 'I'm sorry, Scott, I do love you. I didn't mean all that about bitches and what have you. Truthfully, I'm devastated and didn't want it to end like this.' Katherine put her head back on the chair and closed her eyes. A solitary tear escaped, ran down her cheek and stopped. If she had opened her eyes, another torrent would have followed.

Through the kitchen window, I saw Billy slumped in the driver's seat of his car, head on the backrest, door wide open. I ran out and made him get into the passenger seat. He was crying like his world had collapsed. He was inconsolable for nearly an hour. Katherine leaving him would be his undoing. There was only a flimsy thread of cotton holding him together as it was. She was the only semblance of stability he had. Without her in his life, I couldn't begin to imagine what would happen.

They had met after a Sunday church service because their cars had been blocked in. They'd waited together until everyone left. The conversation ignited the beginning of a romance, and the rest was history. Nothing happened by accident, not even parked cars shunted nose to tail for some reason.

'Can we go for a drink?' Billy asked, sounding like less than half the man he usually was. Billy never asked, he told.

We walked into the Spring Croft Tavern in Baillieston, a place where hitman Billy McPhee, the right-hand man of Tam

'The Licensee' McGraw, was brutally stabbed in the head, body and face. He died while watching the Scotland vs Wales rugby match on the pub TV. A Brewers Fayre was in full swing during the attack, so the place was full of families with children. It was a chilling reminder that when someone came to kill you, they didn't care who else was around. Billy suddenly looked older and weathered. For the first time, he also seemed vulnerable. We had two belts of Scotch and sat in a quiet corner. I began to think it may be wise to leave the whole situation.

Billy seemed calmer when I drove him home. 'Where are you going after you drop me off?' Billy asked. I was planning on going to Laura's house to stay for the night.

'Do you want me to stay with you? I will if you want,' I replied.

'No. I'm alright. I'll relax, get my head down early. This'll blow over. Thanks, Scott.' When we got to his house, I handed him my house keys, gave him a kiss and a hug, like always, and left. As I drove away, I had an uneasy feeling. Something was telling me that something wasn't right. I nearly turned the car around but didn't.

The morning light was streaming through the flimsy curtains when my phone woke me. Laura stirred, stretched like a cat and watched me while running her fingers through her tousled hair to straighten it.

'Hello?'

'Scott?' It was Billy.

'I want to tell you that you're the best friend I ever had. I will always love you. I will see you later.' The phone went dead. A shiver ran down my spine as my body shook. What the fuck was that all about?

I raced for my supercharged Lexus and floored it to Billy's house, 18 miles away. The car slewed sideways as I hit the brakes and stopped just inches short of hitting the house. I jumped out. The door wouldn't open. I searched my pockets and then I remembered that I had given him my keys.

'Billy! Billy!' I yelled through the door.

There was no answer. I spotted a sledgehammer propped up against a wheelbarrow, left behind by the men who'd been laying a stone pathway in the garden. I rushed over to grab it. I hit the bottom right-hand corner of the door and then the top, slung the sledgehammer aside, and kicked the door down.

Billy was hanging by a rope from a beam in the hallway near the black piano with its lid closed. He'd cut into the plaster to expose the beam. His false eye, which never perfectly matched his real one, was still in its socket, thank God. Both his staring eyes looked the same for once – dead and gone. His face was bulging, swollen and purple. His mouth was wide open with saliva on his chin. Had his fake eye fallen out and landed on the scatterings of broken ceiling plaster on the carpet, I would have probably run out of there and never gone back. I might have tried to shove his false eye back into his socket before anyone else turned up. Billy was many things but never a ghoul.

I pulled my lock-back knife out of my pocket and cut him down. I caught him as he fell and toppled over with his weight. I was on the ground, holding him in disbelief.

'Oh, Billy, my friend, what have you done, what have you done? Jesus Christ.' I stayed there motionless with him in my arms for a long time, recollecting everything we'd done and shouldn't have done; all the beating and stabbing, dealing and cheating and ruining lives. I closed my eyes, trying to blank out the dark memories just for a second. In my imagination, Papa walked in, took it in, looked right into me and evaporated. Come back, Papa, I need you.

Lately, I'd seen my grandparents and my mum while presenting more front than Vegas, pretending things were okay. For a long time, I hadn't taken off my coat while visiting, so it was obvious that I never intended staying long. We'd chit-chat while nothing was ever really said. Papa knew what I was doing because, like an American Indian scout, he always had his ear to the ground to hear the rumblings. Reckoned he was biding his time until the storm blew over. I hadn't spoken to him or God in months.

I needed to tell Katherine because she had to hear it from me, but I had no idea where she was. I called her mobile, but it went straight to her answer phone. I left a message, asking her to call me as soon as possible. Then I called Billy's sister, Angela. Fortunately, she did answer.

'Angela, something's happened. You need to come to Billy's house now.'

'What's happened, Scott?'

'Come alone.'

Angela stepped on to the fallen front door, walked in and stopped dead in her tracks. Billy was on the ground with the rope still around his neck. My hands were over my face. I looked at her through the gaps between my fingers. She put her hand to her mouth and screamed so loudly that the chandelier trembled. The tinkling sound of glass filled the room. When she removed her hand, her face was marked where she'd gripped her skin. Two rivers of black mascara began to paint over her red-marked cheeks, then she collapsed with shock.

It took her 15 minutes to gather her senses. Angela called Katherine, then the police. This was all going to take some explaining, and I wasn't in the mood. I wanted to run and disappear off the face of the earth for a few days, but I couldn't let them down. I was suddenly the only man in the house. After Katherine digested the initial shock, she made my choice easy.

'Scott, please stay here with me, at least until after the funeral,' Katherine asked. Her bloodshot eyes, drained of tears, were canvassed by the snow-white color of her sullen face. 'I don't want to be here alone.'

I went back to the house before dark each night for Katherine. We'd sit in the kitchen having supper, which was never anything special. It was just something to eat.

'I blame myself,' she said one night.

'It's not your fault, Kat.'

'Really?' she asked with a hint of sarcasm and exasperation.

'Yes, really. Are you gonna be all right for money?' She nodded.

'I think so. Billy had what he called a rainy-day fund overseas.'

'Funeral arrangements? Can I help with any of that?'

'That's sweet, thank you, but no. It gives me something to do ... Scott?'

'Yes?'

'Thank you for being here. I know you've got a life elsewhere.'

'I wouldn't be anywhere else right now,' I replied.

When I went to bed, I fell asleep to Katherine pacing downstairs. The next day, Pamela moved back to the house to help console her mother. She even tried to console me. Maybe it was Pamela's way of trying to make things right after our mess or with Billy. But it wasn't her fault. I had started it. And Billy loved her in spite of herself. It took one to know one.

Three days after the suicide, Pamela came to my bedroom in the middle of the night, slipped under the white cotton duvet and slid down next to me in the dark. She was in need of warmth; a cuddle, a talk and someone familiar next to her.

'I'm sorry about what happened between us. There's no excuse for it. I was angry and jealous and got carried away.'

'I got carried away, too, and I'm way more to blame than you for all of this. I do wish we had talked before the abortion,' I said quietly. I hadn't mentioned it before.

'David made me. He threatened me, and I believed him. I'm terrified of him,' she said. 'I didn't tell anyone, but it seemed the only thing to do. It will prey on my mind forever. I think Mum knows but refuses to talk about it.'

When Pamela and I slept together in the early days, Billy was always the last one to bed. He'd check the property, turn on the alarms and let the dogs out. We'd hear him walking up the wooden stairs. He'd open our door an inch or two, just to annoy me, then go to his bedroom without closing our door. It was his joke but also a reminder that he was the boss of the house.

In the middle of the night, something woke me. It sounded like someone was in the house. Pamela was asleep, breathing quietly, with her head next to mine. Katherine never went downstairs at night because she didn't want to trigger the alarm by accident. The dogs were out and barking, and I heard footsteps on the stairs. Our bedroom door opened just a fraction. I held my breath and reached for my knife, which I always kept close to hand.

'Bilko, is that you?' I whispered, then drifted back to sleep.

'Did you hear anything in the night?' I asked Pamela the next morning.

'Yes. I didn't say anything. I think Dad was trying to tell us he's still here, watching.'

'Footsteps on the stairs? The steps that creak?'

'Yes, I think so.'

'Did you hear our door open?'

'No. Did you?'

'Must've been a bad dream.'

All day, the open door preyed on my mind, but it wasn't the only thing. Billy had a neighbour named Cal, who lived three doors up the road from Billy's place. Cal was a good-looking fella, so the girls said. He was squeaky clean and fixed electrics for a living. He could turn his hand to anything. Cal liked to hang around with us but without getting into any bother. He typically came to the house because the kitchen electrics were arse about face. Turn the switches off, the electrics work; turn them on, they don't. Cal came over to offer his condolences.

Cal filled a kettle and plugged it in. The plug popped out and landed on the granite kitchen surface. 'I've never seen nothing like that before,' he said, looking puzzled and scratching his head. I don't need this spooky shit, I thought. But Katherine calmly reassured us.

'Don't worry. It takes a while before a spirit crosses over,' she said. Katherine was into all that bollocks, but I was not. I had to get away from the house, so I quickly moved back in with Laura, but still spent most of my time with Katherine.

Being the opened-minded sort, Katherine told me she'd gone to see a spiritualist one day while I was gone. Bollocks or not, I listened politely. Katherine looked a bit spooked. 'She closed the curtains, dimmed the lights to darken the room, lit two candles and closed her eyes for about a minute. Then, suddenly, the room went cold and the candles flickered. There was no wind in there, Scott. Then the lady says, "Watch this piece of paper. Billy wants me to send you a message." With her eyes still tight shut, she drew a triangular Ku Klux Klan mask with eyeholes in it, then wrote down the words "ha ha ha". It was very strange.'

Honestly, that was pure Billy, a devout racist. He was pro-Scotland and anti-the rest of the world. Maybe it was a message from Billy. But I couldn't help but think: Those types of messages could only be portrayed from a person (or spirit) who was in a very unpleasant place. Billy's funeral was also a dark affair. The local priest had been called away at short notice with some family problem, or so we were told. He probably just went on holiday. Priests can be economical with the truth. So, we had to settle for a stand-in. The only person available was a Nigerian preacher who didn't know Billy from a hole in the ground, which is where Billy's body was heading.

The only thing that kept me from becoming uncontrollably emotional was an image I couldn't shake. Any second, I expected the coffin lid to pop open. Billy would jump out, clutching a Glock semi-automatic and ready to pull the trigger. This particular House of God had every villain inside it, including Campbell, who'd done 18 years for the Ice Cream Wars, Joe Steel the Enforcer and Big Alex Morrison, along with his gang of boxers and scrap gatherers.

I sat next to Paddy Mullen, who had a gun tucked in his trousers. I knew because I could see the end of the butt. He tapped me on the arm to get my attention and leaned over. 'Guys here are gonna make a move on you. There's bad blood, Scott. Billy died leaving a big debt.' Every time we stood up and sat down, I was thinking his gun was going to go off and shoot him in the leg. I didn't want any commotion. Not today of all days. The funeral was hard enough without a gunfight breaking out.

'Is the safety on?' I whispered, smiling.

'I hope so. It's got a hair trigger and a mind of its own,' he smiled back.

After the funeral, close family attended the burial, then we all headed off to Shettleston Social Club. The place was back in Billy's territory, so I felt more comfortable. Katherine had organised it superbly well, so there was enough food and drink to feed the town. Anything left over went straight over to God's waiting room, where Billy used to go and help out the old folks. That was in his will of wishes. His favourite old gal, Mary, wasn't there any more. I was at the bar waiting to be handed a double Scotch when Moiffy pitched up out of the blue.

'Scott …'

'Hey, a miracle you're still alive. Have a drink, pal.'

'I'm sorry I fucked up. I took off. Billy would have eventually killed me.' I handed him my glass of Scotch. He drained it in one hit. 'See you, Scott.' Moiffy left the crowded room. I watched the door open and close. Maybe he'd just come for some reassurance that I wasn't going to finish off Billy's business, but it was too late for all that. Billy was gone.

I had just turned around to talk to Katherine when 'Stone Cold' Joe Doods, who nobody in their right mind fucked with, came over.

'I'm sorry for your loss. I know you and Billy were best mates, but there's a problem.'

'I know, but I don't need this now.'

'Actually, Scott, you do. Big Chap Buford wants the money Billy owes him. It's fifty grand.'

'Or else wha?' Joe didn't say anything. He didn't need to.

I looked across the room and saw Buford looking in my direction. Fuck, I didn't need this shit now. But, I decided if he wasn't coming to me, I would go to him. We called him Buford because he was crazy like Buford 'Mad Dog' Tannen, the Wild West gunfighter. He also had Lee Van Cleef's rattlesnake eyes, which darted behind his big eyeglasses.

'Sorry Billy ended up this way,' he said. I sat down and nodded.

'Aye. We agree about that.' He moved closer.

'If you don't get that fucking money, Scott, I'm gonna do Billy's wife, his kin, then you. Let's just say, there's a lot hanging on it,' he said. The joke fucked with me, but I said nothing and steadied my temper. Like in the ring, I just held his stare without blinking. I wanted to blow him a kiss but didn't.

Buford had a younger brother named Tam. We used to call them Big Specky and Wee Specky because they both wore their stupid eyeglasses. I found out later that Tam had gone to visit Katherine at home. Good thing for him I wasn't there. I would've nailed the bastard. Tam had threatened her, giving Katherine a two-week deadline to repay the debt.

Katherine already blamed herself for Billy's death. Now she was afraid she'd soon have her family and me on her conscience as well. She wasn't sleeping. Billy wouldn't have wanted any of this. I needed to figure out where to find the money in two weeks. Katherine mentioned selling the house. Over my dead body.

I would've called the Bowers brothers, who might have helped me out. But all three brothers were doing time for the Gatwick airport robbery. Decent plan. With the intention of just walking out with the money, they used a fake Brinks Mat van and bogus uniforms, along with a set of bogus documents and identities. They would've got away with it, too, but their headquarters had been under surveillance for months leading up to the robbery.

I came up with a plan myself, but it was a long shot. It was complicated, involving calling in a lot of favours and debts, endless wheels within wheels and driving to London. I wasn't exactly happy about any of it but had to do what I could. Fifty grand was a lot of money. I could flog my cars and watches and beg and borrow to raise nearly 20 grand easily and quickly, but 50 grand was another matter.

I called a good pal, Danny, and explained the situation to him. He told me he had a mate called Winker, an old-school professional thief with a good record as an accomplished safe cracker. To help collect funds, Danny told me that I may be able to recover a big debt for Winker from a pub owner named Barry. It was a generous offer but with strings attached. There always were. I needed a quick and short-term fix, though. I'd worry about the later-on consequences later on.

So, mission Probably Impossible meant going to London to get the dough. The debt Winker needed to collect was being held in a massive safe, which you could only open with Semtex, the safe's combination or by persuasion. He knew Barry had a ton of folding somewhere and the dough would be somewhere where he's never very far away – his pub.

The quick solution would've been to take care of Buford, which I wasn't too opposed to. Every night, Buford could be found at a Glasgow golf club bar between 6pm and 8pm. I drove there and looked everywhere for him, but that night it was my bad luck and his good luck that nobody had seen him. So, there was no alternative with time running out – next stop, London.

I'd met this Barry when I was working with the Bowers brothers, so I wasn't a complete stranger. Otherwise, I'd never been able to make contact. Barry owned a big pub near Charing Cross and was usually in the company of Freddie Foreman, Frankie Fraser, Tony Lambrianou and that gang. They haunted white-collar boxing show dinners and nightclubs. Danny had given me his number, so I called the pub and he answered the phone. 'Hello? This is Barry.'

'Hello, Barry, it's Scott Dixon. I met you with Martin and Paul and the lads a few years back.'

'Oh yeah, Scott, I remember you. How you doing?'

'Where you gonna be tonight? I thought I'd look you up for old times.'

'I'll be here in the bar tonight. Come along.'

I had a 9mm with a silencer and a spare clip, a folded-up black bin bag, a pair of handcuffs and a roll of black tape in my pockets. I didn't know if I was on a fool's errand or not, but I would find out soon enough. I wore a long, black leather coat and a flat cap, and before the heat I had a few whiskies to warm up. Failure was not an option. My best pal's family was in trouble, and so was I, so I couldn't take no for an answer.

I got to the bar and saw Barry behind it. He was planting a bottle of Scotch into an optic. He had his back to me but, overweight and virtually bald, he had an unmistakable stature.

'Hi, Barry, how you doin', pal?' He turned around and recognised me straightaway.

'Oh, Scotty boy, you haven't changed. What are you drinking, son?' I hated being called Scotty, especially by a Cockney twat like him.

'Can I have a private word first, but not here?'

'Okay.'

'Sam, watch the bar, will you? I'll be back in ten minutes,' he said to the only other person behind the bar. It was still early, and the place was mostly empty.

Barry unlocked a door marked 'Private' and we walked into his back office. It was full of empty spirit and wine boxes. Behind an old desk littered with papers, I saw an iron safe. After eyeing it, I put one arm around his back and stuck the piece down his jacket, right into his bollocks.

'Listen …' he protested.

'Listen, you. I'm here to collect, and you know who for. Open it.'

He turned and looked at me. His eyes told me he knew I meant business. I pushed him towards the big, cast-iron safe, which had two combination locks on it and was cemented into the floor. No wonder nobody had nicked it. You would've needed a road drill.

'I'll give you what's in here, then you're dead,' Barry said, fumbling with the locks. 'It's not only my money in here. You're taking from a fucking army. You know who I know,

Dixon. You're fucked, Dixon. They'll boil you alive, and I'll be watching.'

'Well, you know who I know, and they'll be watching *you*,' I said. 'Buford sent me.'

'Buford? Buford who? Look, I'll give you one chance to walk out of here. Do you wanna take it?'

I looked him in the eyes. 'No.' He turned back around and opened the safe. Inside, it looked like the Bank of England. No point in being greedy. 'Fifty or a bullet?' I snapped. He pulled out 50 wads of notes with rubber bands around them, then prised himself up from the floor. 'Sit down,' I said. He sat on a chair, and I handcuffed him, taped his mouth and left. Sam the barman was busy chatting up a bird and didn't see me leave.

To make the getaway as fast as possible, I hailed a black cab and leapt in the back. I clutched the stuffed bin bag until I was dropped off next to my car in Soho Square. I grabbed a burger from a place at the top of Dean Street, washed it down with a soda, called it a day and slept in the car. Having that much cash in the car was risky, but I was armed.

I slept longer than I had wanted and woke up to a parking ticket on my windscreen – evidence I'd been here. I drove back to Scotland watching the speedometer like a hawk, never going over 70mph. I stopped for fuel once, paid cash, grabbed a coffee, downed it and carried on. I got back to Hamilton just as the streetlights were turning back on and called Katherine's mobile.

'Kat, you all okay?'

'Yeah.'

'Okay, we'll talk later.'

I called Buford's mobile.

'Yeah.'

'Want the money?'

'Where?'

'By Billy's gravestone, so he can watch me hand it to you personally. Come alone.'

The churchyard was pitch black and silent. I shone a torch to make sure I'd gotten the right gravestone and dropped the black bag next to it. 'Hi Billy pal, I hope you're okay. This is to make sure nobody bothers your family.' After dropping the money, I slunk into the shadows and found a place, out of sight, behind a big yew tree. After not too long, I saw a car pull up by the gates with the headlights switched off. I saw three torches leading three people, then suddenly realised that Buford might not know where Billy's grave was. Bugger, I hadn't thought of that.

'I know about where it is. I watched the funeral from a ways,' a voice said. Thank God for that. They disappeared as quickly as they had arrived. Job done. While that had taken care of the situation, Buford was a name that Barry wouldn't soon forget. I waited for about a half an hour, then legged it to mine and drove away. Before I went to see Katherine the next day, I stopped by a travel agency to get some holiday brochures about Egypt. I thought it might give her something to look forward to. She probably wouldn't go any time soon, but maybe some day.

Round 9

Out of the Frying Pan...

June 2006

I had good reasons to go to Malta. Like a proper Shirley Valentine, Mum had gone there not long ago. She didn't fall in love with anyone but did immediately fall in love with the island. Compared to grey, drizzly, bleak, introverted and unemployed Scotland, Malta was sunny, vibrant, outgoing and outdoors, with the opportunity for work if you wanted it. It was a new life versus an old one – absolutely no contest.

I flew over with a triple agenda. Firstly, I wanted to make sure Mum was okay. Secondly, I wanted to check it out to see if Laura might like it. I needed a fresh start and a new life myself. Mum was as brown as a berry. She'd put on a bit of weight, which she needed, and she was happy and chirpy. I'd not seen her look so well in ages.

There was also a growing boxing scene in Malta and while it was still in its infancy, it had strong roots. The island was becoming a new place for promising boxers to train and fight.

Over the years, I had promised myself I'd open a gym and Malta didn't seem like the worst home for it. With mostly clear skies and warm temperatures, the weather also got a big tick.

Mum showed me around, leaving virtually no place unvisited. It was an island of great contrasts. Reflected in its architecture and people, Malta had a chequered history marked by endless invasions, making a liquorice of an all-sorts variety. Late one night, after the tourists had left, we went to Mdina, known as the Silent City, and explored its golden, sand-coloured walls and winding narrow alleyways. The silence was ethereal and religious, as if you were sitting inside a deserted cathedral with its doors closed. People lived here, presumably in silence without having sex or arguments.

'You get fined if you so much as sneeze here,' she whispered.

'You wha?' I shouted.

'Shhh.'

Malta also offered a range of very expensive and very cheap restaurants, satisfying every taste and budget. Mum knew the manager of the Rendevous, a restaurant on the waterfront. We were treated to a free lunch and I'd never tasted food like it. Unfortunately, there were only a few beaches on the island. Xlendi had a small, sandy beach and it was a popular diving site, judging by the amount of scuba gear strewn everywhere.

One day, we went over to Gozo, Malta's sister island. Just half an hour away on the ferry, Gozo was a good getaway from Malta and very quiet. But the area that caught my eye, not far from where Mum lived, was St Julian's. Offering a bit of everything, St Julian's was a microcosm of the island – a mishmash of old and new architecture and thinking. It was situated on the harbour, with restaurants and bars occupying every available inch of ground. Attractive and relaxing on one hand, St Julian's was also exciting and a bit crazy on the other. A short, uphill walk from the harbour was one of the maddest streets I'd ever been on, with countless bars and clubs offering all-night-long fun, games and opportunities.

Along with the island's history, weather, natural beauty and culture, I also couldn't help but notice the women. Everywhere I looked, there were hundreds upon hundreds of women, most of them very tasty. After visiting for a few days, I began to think that this was a place I should definitely come to live – alone.

I rang Laura.

'Hello.'

'Fancy a change of scene?'

'What's it like?'

'Better than Hamilton.'

'In what way?'

'In every way.'

So, Laura and I decided to up sticks and move with her two kids and our baby to Malta. Just like that.

It was the perfect time for us to move as things had been getting hot in Hamilton. Laura's first two children were with someone else and she conceived our son, Toby, while she was still with him. Needless to say, he didn't appreciate it. In the two weeks before I left for Malta, both of my cars had been bashed and torched: a 4x4 and a BMW convertible. Maybe him, maybe not. I couldn't say for certain. But I suspected it. The 4x4 was no big deal, but I was fucked off about the BMW, which I loved.

I saw the whole event as a sign. When someone starts igniting your motors, you can't help but wonder what, or who, may be next. It was definitely time to wave goodbye to bonny Scotland for a wee bit, if not for a long while. My grandparents could always fly over for a holiday in the sun, so we weren't cutting ties, just expanding opportunities. Malta was only three hours from Glasgow airport. It took longer to go to London by train. And if we wanted or needed to, we could always pop back home.

After flying back to Scotland to sort some things, I returned to Malta alone. I wanted to set up a living arrangement for Laura before she arrived. I left Glasgow in 15°C of gloom and looked forward to the sunny prospect of 30°C on arrival. On the plane, I sat next to a bird named Tracy from Cardiff, who told me she was afraid of flying. I didn't share that I was afraid of flying, too. I told her about Laura, our baby on the way and the life I was looking forward to in Malta. In my experience, women loved all this. She had taken a job with HSBC in Malta and already had her apartment sorted.

Tracy was beautifully and expensively dressed in a buttoned-up kind of way. Not the kind of clothes you'd normally wear to fly in. Dressed like she was on a date, Tracy couldn't have been more than 5ft 3in, but she was tidy with it. We eventually got tucked into a deeper conversation.

'Where are you staying?' Tracy asked, biting her lip. It was a definite invitation for me to examine the goods. She ran her fingers through her hair and shook her head back while waiting for my reply. There was a moment's silence.

'At yours, if you're up for it.'

So, I hit Malta with a bang. Trouble was, Mum was coming to get me from the airport. With Laura about to have my baby and her grandchild, Mum would've gone nuts if she'd seen me with another bird. I dodged seeing Mum, and Tracy and I grabbed a taxi. Next morning, I switched on my phone and saw eight messages from my mother. I took a deep breath and called her.

'Sorry, Mum. I missed the flight and caught another one. I'm on the way to your place now, so see you in half an hour.'

There were no planes arriving in Malta from Glasgow at the time. My lie wouldn't have make an ounce of itinerary sense, if Mum had checked. I made up a different pack of lies to Laura. I knew she and my mum wouldn't talk. At the time, they didn't get on that well. But Mum was very excited about the baby, no matter who was carrying it, so she would be tight lipped with Laura for the time being.

I arrived in Malta with a few quid I'd saved up, so there was no need to work for a while, but Mum had different plans for me. She worked as an organiser for an open-top bus sightseeing company. Through a few contacts, she lined up a job for me selling timeshare properties. What did I know about timeshares? Fortunately, I didn't have to sell anything. I just drove a timeshare rep named Julie around to look for potential victims. She was a natural at spotting people who appeared to have cash. For every potential customer we got through the door, we earned €100. So, we set ourselves a target of four victims a day, then called it a day and went to party.

In September, I found a furnished apartment that overlooked St Julian's harbour, and Laura flew over with her boys. To turn it into more of a home, with a bigger TV, new sofas and toys for the boys, I had earned extra cash by occasionally working security at a strip bar, or so-called gentlemen's club. Every night, the place was packed full of animals and filled with temptations. But that gig didn't last long. I was sick of doing the kind of work that placed me in the middle of trouble. I was trying to turn my life around. Laura loved the apartment and thought Malta was paradise. It was definitely a far cry from home, where police sirens wailed and scallies hung on every street corner making trouble.

My baby boy arrived at St Luke's on 2 October at 11pm. As he was emerging into the world, I was in top spirits and humming 'Hey Jude', so we decided to call him Toby Jude Dixon. Papa and Gran were thrilled to bits with the news and the name. For two months after his birth, life was nearly perfect. Holding Toby and trying to figure out who he resembled most was like a dream. Being with him gave me more pleasure than I'd ever experienced. I'd look into his eyes for ages while holding him in silence and listening to his quiet breathing. It was a wondrous thing – beyond words, fear, regret, hopes or memories.

Sometimes, I would put my ear a millimetre from his mouth to feel the reassurance of his warm breath, just to make sure he was still alive. People told me this was normal parent behaviour, especially with their firstborn. I felt we had connected in a way I couldn't explain. For once, I felt completely at peace and balanced. I was his protector; he was my saviour. I wondered if this was how my father felt when I was born. The question only flashed in my head, then quickly vanished.

We had a great Christmas together with Mum and the boys but by the end of January, things had started to slide. Laura gave me a lot of cold shoulder, both in the day and especially in bed at night. She wouldn't let me anywhere near her. This was coupled with a lot of, what seemed to me, unjustified verbal abuse. I didn't know what had triggered it. Maybe it was postnatal depression, which was a tricky thing for me to get my head around. I didn't know if it was temporary, permanent or something else. I just felt her mood was my fault. I began to feel depressed and worried I was heading for another collision course. Fortunately, Julie came to my rescue and kept me buoyant.

'It must be hormones. Having a baby takes a lot out of you. You couldn't really understand but she'll come back to her senses and everything will return to normal,' she assured me. After a profitable day, we went out for a drink and I poured my heart out to her. The more I revealed, the closer we got.

'Come here,' she said. She put her arms around me, looked into my eyes and I kissed her.

'I've been hoping you would do that for months,' she smiled. 'Let's go back to yours.'

This went on for weeks, turning into a full-blown affair. I couldn't carry on with the deceit, so I told Laura what had been going on. She attacked me, like a wild cat, scratching my face. I left before I did something stupid, then I moved out. The biggest blow was leaving Toby. I didn't contact Laura for two weeks, then called to say I was coming over to get my clobber. 'What took you so long? It's been packed up for a week.' She sounded cool on the phone, not hysterical like usual. It was too composed, and I wondered what she was up to. I still had a key, so we arranged a time for me to go to the apartment when nobody was there. I picked up my suitcases, put the key on the hall table and left.

I was going to a party that night with Julie and she asked me to make a special effort. A lot of her friends would be there. Julie was in the shower when I opened the first suitcase. Every bit of clothing I owned had been cut into pieces; even my Guccis were slashed to bits. The only clothing not ruined was the tracksuit I was wearing.

Laura quickly pulled down the shutters, refusing me access to Toby. Then the situation went from bad to worse. After a while, she didn't answer my calls. I began to feel desperate and regretful for leaving Toby. I wondered if my father had felt like this when he deserted us. Maybe, one day, I'd ask him.

When Julie and I went out on Saturday nights, we'd often stay out until dawn. On one rare occasion, we called it a night at 2am and headed for bed. At 5am, my mobile rang. It was

Tony Lee, an old mate from back home. I knew something must be wrong.

'Yeah, Tony, what's up?'

'Have you seen the papers?'

'What papers?'

'The *News of the World* papers.'

'Tony, how the fuck would I see the *News of the World* in the middle of the night in Malta?'

'I advise you to get up and find a copy somehow. They must've come in on the last plane. It's about you – a love rat in Malta. There's a picture of you and Laura.'

'Okay, thanks. I'll get back to you.'

'Who was that?' asked Julie, still half asleep.

'My pal Tony from back home. He's just messing about. Said he was in a garage buying ciggies and decided to call me. He never could tell the time.'

I went back to sleep and woke again to my phone at 7.30am. I needed to switch it off. This was getting ridiculous.

'Hello, son ...'

'Hey, Papa, you okay?'

'Yes. Get a copy of the *News of the World*. Laura must've given them a story about you. It's not good. I thought you should know, if you don't already.'

Five minutes after I hung up the phone with Papa, my phone rang again. This time it was a reporter from *The Sun*. 'Do you want to reply to the story in the *News of the World*? We'd like to hear your side of the story, Scott.'

'No, fuck off.'

I got dressed, drove to the nearest shop and bought the paper. There it was: Scott Dixon, the love rat, and Laura, the victim. How could she have done this? Airing our dirty laundry in public? Later, I heard she'd been paid £5,000 but the story was complete shit. The worst part of the story was her claim that I wasn't keeping up with maintenance payments. There *were* two sides to that story. I was making payments but had been late a few times. For that, she had a point, though she hadn't shared her story with the world to receive payment from me. She just wanted revenge and to publicly humiliate me, which took some doing. Sticks and stones may break my bones, but words … As a matter of fact, words *can* hurt. She was still the mother of my child and Toby was still my world. Regardless, I felt my level of distrust rise after the situation.

Three months before the *News of the World* story, Julie had sold a boat for a client, Ian, who'd promised her €3,000 in commission. She still hadn't been paid a cent, although the boat had been sold and paid for. I could tell it had stayed on her mind because it was often on her lips. Enough of this. I knew this Ian fella, so I phoned him.

'Hello Ian, it's Scott Dixon. You owe Julie money, you know how much. I'm coming to get it tomorrow at your office at noon, so you'd better have it.' Like a flash, he agreed and apologised, making some excuse about his mother being ill and the normal bullshit that liars spouted. Job done.

'How can I possibly repay you?' she asked. Another satisfied client.

Two days later, I was drinking beer and chasers and chewing on nuts at Munchies, an upstairs bar in Bugibba, trying to get my money back from a one-armed bandit that had just robbed me blind. Finally, I kicked the machine so hard that it buzzed a few times and died. Before I could complain to the bar manager, trouble walked in through the door.

'Who's this cunt Scott Dixon, anyone know him?' shouted a loud-mouth Cockney who'd just swaggered in.

'Hey, can I help you?' I asked. He looked like he'd had a few, which was always a basic mistake, especially if you were looking for trouble. All mouth and trousers with small hands, he looked like an idiot, too.

'You sound Scottish, mate. Where can I find this Dixon arsehole?' I turned around and everyone in the bar was looking at me. I was somewhat a regular at the place, so they knew me. I ran my finger across my lips to keep everyone quiet.

'He phoned my mate, Ian, and threatened him. Made him hand over a lot of money, but I'm gonna sort him out and get the cash back.' He blathered on until he hiccupped. Oh boy. This guy had already had too much to drink, behaving and mouthing like a shit-shot cowboy who couldn't hit a barn door with a shotgun. One punch would do it.

'Let me buy you a pint, my friend. But first, let's go outside and phone this silly cunt. I've got his number,' I said. Towards the bottom of the stairs, I quickly spun around and caught him clean with a half-powered uppercut. His eyes rolled back into his head like a fruit machine rocking up the result. He went out cold and crashed a bit down the stairs. I dragged him by his ankles and dumped him next to a massive wheelie bin. I would have dumped him in it, but the bin was full of rubbish already. Half an hour later, he came wobbling back into the bar.

'What for?' he asked, nursing his chin with his right hand.

'Because I'm Scott Dixon, you silly cunt.' He got the picture and left. I never saw him again.

That was the same day I meet Johnny Essex from Essex, an old guy who resembled Sid James with a purple nose that betrayed his quiet fondness for rum. He said he was a promoter, so I took him at his word. We decided to put on a boxing show at the Sky Club. I would headline while Johnny would match all the undercard fighters with lads from Manchester. Easy. The event would pay a few quid for a few minutes' work.

My real dad actually came over to watch the fight. I didn't see him that often, but we kept in touch in a fairly long-distance sort of way. We normally got on okay. He had done pretty well for himself over the years. He had a couple of good businesses, made good money (not that he'd ever given me any) and drove a Porsche 911. We also had one thing in common. We were both equally partial to single malt. I was never in two minds about my father. I was only ever in one. As far as I was concerned, he had dumped my mum and I had always been an appendage. Another burden, that's all. He'd told her that he hadn't been ready to settle down with a wife and a child. We were no more than a deduction to his drinking fund. Papa was my father as far as I was concerned, but I couldn't help feeling a connection with my real father. Even if it was just a curiosity sort of thing, over the years, when he would talk, I would normally listen.

By staying in touch with him, I think I was always looking for the similarities and differences between us, if there were any. Over the years, as regular as every Saturday night, he would call me. He was always drunk and unable to speak properly. Normally, he'd make another excuse about abandoning us, then have the audacity to tell me he loved me. Maybe he did. Half of me related to the whole thing, while the other half didn't know what to make of it.

Me and my dad were sitting in a little bar called Miracles and we'd had a few belts when four boys I knew came in.

'Good luck tonight, Scott. We'll be there,' one of them said.

'Where?'

'You know, your fight.'

'That's tomorrow … on Saturday.'

'It's Saturday today, mate.' Fuck. It was just after 7pm and the first fight was in an hour. I was already lagged. I downed four pints of water, not that it would make much difference, and grabbed my dad.

'Come on. Let's get the show on the road,' I said.

I changed as fast as I could, still wobbly from the booze. Smelling of Scotch and sweat, I didn't bother putting on my boxing boots, since I would've had trouble with the laces. So, when I climbed through the ropes, I was still wearing my trainers. For a second, it looked like I was about to fight two opponents. I shook my head, punched myself on the chest and single vision returned in the nick of time. Otherwise, I'd have been punching thin air. The only way through this shit was to get it over fast. I hoped I didn't get caught. But, as it turned out, that looked unlikely.

In the first round, my opponent ran around the ring to avoid me, which wasn't a bad strategy. I was too pissed to run after him. He tried to throw a punch and missed. That's when I knew he was useless. The round ended, and I collapsed on to my chair feeling sick. Johnny came over to me.

'You're obviously pissed as a rat, Scott, but you can beat this guy easy. Just get on with it, for Christ's sake.' In round two, he came at me fast and ran into a straight right, hit the canvas and stayed there. Job done. I couldn't have gone on much longer.

I climbed out of the ring and saw my dad clutching two Budweisers.

'Here, this one's for you. Well done. Let's go back to the bar, shall we?'

When we arrived, I saw Laura sitting alone at a table by the door. She looked like she'd seen a ghost.

'No need to say anything, I understand,' I said. A Maltese-looking guy came over carrying two drinks.

'Oh, this is Scott,' she said. His face dropped and so did one of the glasses he was carrying. I left them, while he picked up the broken glass, to join Dad at the bar. Seeing Laura reminded me of Toby. Should I talk to my dad about this? Nah, what would he know? I needed to figure it out for myself.

In August of 2009, I fulfilled my life-long dream of opening my own gym. Located on St Julian's harbour, the Lord's Gym was 2,000 square feet of possibilities that overlooked the sea. The gym had all the gear and a ring. It was a general fitness place, as well as a boxing and martial arts gym, so it attracted all sorts. One of my first clients, a guy named Kevin Sammut, bought a six-month membership and paid up front in cash. He looked like a wrong 'un through and through. I could always smell them a mile off. Kevin soon confirmed the smell.

'Look, Scott. When I go out, I sometimes carry large amounts of cash and don't wanna get turned over. I just need someone to watch my back. I'll pay you well,' he said. It didn't seem like a huge deal, but I did shadow him in some pretty dark places. Nothing much ever happened trouble-wise because people generally avoided me, but I could see how he made his money. I'd given that up long ago. After all, I had the gym to run and it didn't take long for it to take off.

One day, without applying for it, I became the Maltese Olympic national team boxing coach. I was probably the one person on the island with the experience and credentials for the job. We went to Milan for the AIBA World Boxing Championship. In many ways, it was just like the Olympics. It was a big knockout competition with fanfare and all the razzmatazz. When we walked on to the floor, there were three of us waving Maltese flags. I looked up at the jumbo screen and realised, for the first time, that not one of us was Maltese. Our hopeful, Haithem Lamouz, was Tunisian but because he lived in Malta, he qualified. I was Scottish and the other fella, Joe Higgs, was a Scouser. My boy exited in the second round but he put on a good show.

But preying on my mind, constantly, was the phone call I'd received from Papa while in Milan. He told me that he'd been getting calls.

'Is someone bothering you, Papa?' He didn't answer the question, so I knew. The others flew back to Malta and I took a plane to Glasgow to stay with my grandparents for two days. Papa told me what had been going down. He'd been receiving phone calls with implied threats, as well as some unwelcome visits. We decided to disappear to Oban on the west coast of Scotland for a few days to stay with my mum's sister, Auntie Jennifer. She'd been living in Oban since she was 19 years old.

In the past, we had spent a bit of time together. Auntie Jennifer had left Hamilton for a job at the Caledonian Hotel. She got a one-way train ticket, and that was that. She started work as a chambermaid, then receptionist and worked her way up the ladder. After 30 years, she left to run Aulay's Pub, where she enjoyed a piece of the action. Jennifer had got married and had two kids, Grant and Denise. When she was a kid, Auntie Jennifer visited Oban with Papa, Gran and Mum for the summer holidays. Every time she went there, she never wanted to leave. She had been destined to live there. Over the years, Papa watched her grow up from a distance and checked on her welfare. Needless to say, Papa had a lot of friends in Oban. Not much went on in Oban but it was a place I knew well. A little fishing village with only one policeman, where people could tell the time by the tide, Oban was full of fond memories and familiar faces. If anyone was after me, they wouldn't look for me there.

Nothing much had changed over the years. My auntie still lived in the same house, which featured grey-stone walls and a slate roof that was always smeared with white seagull shit. Auntie Jennifer took after Gran more than Papa. She didn't have his mad shock of ringlets hair. She had dead-straight, neat-cut blonde hair and was skinny like Mum. She was also fond of me, I could always tell that. When I was younger, she would make me something to eat, make sure I washed properly and brushed my teeth. Then, she'd tuck me up in bed and make sure I said my prayers.

During one trip, Papa drove Mum, Gran and me to Oban in his powder-blue Ford Escort. Papa loved that car and drove it slowly to Oban. I used to think he drove slowly to save petrol, but that was never the reason. 'I'm always driving to a schedule normally. It's good to take my time once in a while,' he said. 'Taking things slowly is part of going on holiday, so is taking in the countryside.' We listened to Nat King Cole while taking in the pastoral surroundings, then stopped for a picnic lunch that Gran had prepared. She laid out a tartan rug and we tucked into sausage rolls and sandwiches and drank tea. Papa picked some heather and put one piece on the front of the car, like a badge, and gave another piece to Gran.

'Heather is lucky,' she said while pinning the purple flower on to her coat lapel.

'We're in God's country now, Scott,' Papa said. 'I often think I would've liked to have lived here, not just visited. One day Jean and I might just move to Oban. Spend the rest of our days living amongst good friends. Just peace and quiet.' Papa had also visited Oban when he was a boy, so he was carrying on the family tradition by taking me there. 'You may think there's not much to do there, Scott, but there is. You'll see. Open your mind, laddie, to see what's there.'

'Has Auntie Jennifer got a TV?' I asked.

'Yes,' Papa replied, 'but you won't be watching it. There's more to see in Oban than on any TV.'

The first time I visited Oban, I quickly noticed how different it was to Hamilton. There were no burnt-out cars or kids hanging on street corners making bother. There was no litter anywhere and hardly any noise. Just the sound of the sea and boat engines and hundreds of seagulls cawing and squawking. It was a picture postcard kind of place and a little bit unreal compared to where I lived. I got to know the local lads pretty fast and one of them, Peter Laird, dared me to climb up the cliff face and steal a seagull's egg. 'Everyone has to do it,' he said.

I got halfway up the cliff, grabbed a light-brown egg with dark-brown spots on it and waved it at the lads down below. A seagull flew at me, scratched my face, and I dropped the egg while scrambling down the cliff. It was more than a dare, though, it was an initiation.

'So, everyone has to do that?' I asked Peter, who was standing with two other lads I'd met, Scott McCallum and Jimmy Dunn. They just laughed.

'Nobody does that. Not since Willie McTavish fell off the cliff and broke both his legs.'

'Are you kidding me?' I said, wiping the blood off my cheek with my right hand.

'No, but you'll probably be a legend around here by tomorrow.'

While in Oban, I could tell how happy Papa was that I was reliving his own childhood experience. 'Papa, I climbed halfway up a cliff and got a seagull egg.'

'I can see you did. It's written all over your face. Good for you, son. But don't do it again. Once is plenty enough.' Gran cleaned up my face with TCP, which stung like mad and reeked of hospitals.

The other Seagull I got to know was the engine on the back of a small wooden boat called *Daisy May*. It belonged to a friend of my auntie's. Papa showed me how it worked and when the weather was calm, he would let me take it out around the harbour and a little way out to sea. Even though it had oars, in case the engine conked out, Papa always stood and watched until I got back.

We used to snorkel, too, in the hope of nabbing a big crab. It was a profitable enterprise if you caught one. The local restaurants would pay you handsomely – at least £1 or more. Of course, the best plan would've been to motor out to where the lobster pots were marked and nick some lobsters, but Papa told me never to do that. He reminded me that people's lives depended on what they caught, and survival hereabouts was a touch-and-go situation for many.

After weeks of snorkelling, boating and running around with the local lads, it was finally time to go home. As we drove up the hill out of Oban, I looked out of the car's back window on to the village below and wish we could've stayed. Gran turned to me. 'I'm so glad you've had such a lovely time. Do you know, in all these weeks, you haven't watched the television once?'

That was all a long time ago now, but those summer holidays were really good, and the memories always remained hard-etched in my brain. Now being back in Oban, I couldn't help but think that life had turned out a good deal more difficult than I had imagined as a lad. I was sitting in Aulay's Bar in Airds Crescent, Auntie Jennifer's place, having drinks with old friends, cousins and locals. I was amongst a bunch of weather-beaten faces ready to back me up if trouble walked in. Aulay's Bar also served the best haddock and chips in Scotland.

The bar was a warm, friendly place. It was wall to wall with old maritime prints and paintings, charting Oban's seafaring heritage, with an array of telescopes and ships in bottles, oil lamps and all that nautical stuff. Oban was a world away from Hamilton. It was too quiet for me to stay long but great at that moment. It was a place where I could drop my guard and ease off the gas.

Soon after we had arrived, I got a phone call from Malta. Kevin had been arrested and charged with bringing in the biggest marijuana haul ever to land in Malta. I didn't know why someone had bothered to call me. Whatever Sammut had done didn't have anything to do with me, but he had always been a tricky customer. After a while, Papa decided to drive back to Hamilton because Gran wasn't feeling well. He was going to spend the night at his home, then bring her back to Oban if she felt up to it. That night, I went out with my cousin, Denise, to a club, where the theme for the evening was the 80s, so all the birds dolled up to match the music. I met a stunner called Jacqueline who, after a few dances and a bit of a kiss and cuddle, I got back to my aunt's place and into bed.

Around 6am the next day, I heard a loud bang downstairs, followed by the sound of footsteps running up the staircase. My bedroom door flew open, and three big guys wearing suits charged in. The pricks from Glasgow had come to execute me. Jacqueline screamed as they grabbed me. They seized Jacqueline and dumped her on the floor like a sack of potatoes. One big ape pinned me down on my neck with his knees. They put tie-straps around my wrists and ankles and carried me down the stairs, banging my head on the banisters intentionally.

With one hand in between her legs and her other arm covering her tits, Jacqueline watched the commotion from the landing. All I was wearing was a pair of underpants, which I luckily had on because I got up in the night for a slash. Otherwise, I would've been bollock naked. Once we got outside, they bundled me into the back of a police van. They weren't the pricks from Glasgow.

'Are you Scott Dixon?' asked one of the men, showing me a photocopied picture of my face.

'What the fuck's going on? I want my clothes, you cunts.' He looked again at the photocopy and then at me.

'You're under arrest for drug trafficking. Anything you say …' While he read me my rights, one of the other cops went back into the house and came back with my jeans and leather jacket and threw them at me.

'You've got the wrong person. And where's my shirt and shoes, you flathead?'

'Tell that to the judge and fuck your shoes. You've got all you're getting.'

'How did you know I was here?'

'Mobile phone voice recognition,' one cop said with a smile. 'Blame modern technology, you twat.' These bastards had all the gadgets.

Thankfully, Auntie Jennifer had been away for the night. This scene would've upset her deeply. I certainly owed her a new front door, though, if not a lot more. Oban wasn't used to all this disruption and it must've seemed that the wrong side of Glasgow had come to visit. Auntie Jennifer would soon hear about the morning's commotion at her home. What a fucking mess-up this was. The cop slammed the door and I heard it self-lock. Without socks or shoes, I got dressed as much as I could. For once in my life, I hadn't done anything wrong, but these jokers thought otherwise.

The van drove off with police cars flanking in front and behind. This was serious shit. Riding in the back of the police van, I was thankful and relieved that Papa hadn't been here. It would've cut him to the quick. I also had my mind on Gran. I didn't know if she was alright and I was in no position to find out. It took three hours to get to Edinburgh Sheriff Court. The judge read out the list of charges, which sounded like they were for Tony Soprano. In Scotland, you had one chance at a High Court bail but not with this list of charges.

I was taken down to the cells below the courthouse and told to wait for the prison bus. A cop, with a scar down his right cheek, came up to me and smiled. 'All set for your road trip? It's a five-star hotel with communal showers, you Glaswegian cunt. I bet you'll like your new nickname, Ben Dover.'

'Fuck you. I'm from Hamilton, you ignorant pig. If I wasn't cuffed, I'd drop you in one and give you a proper kicking!' He reached for his baton but stopped short of whacking me. The door opened just in the nick of time.

'Dixon, you're on the bus,' yelled someone holding a clipboard.

'Stick that baton up your arse, you pansy.'

Built in a hurry at the beginning of the last century, to house the ever-increasing number of criminals, Edinburgh jail was one of the worst places on earth. Segregated, the jail held killers in one part, paedophiles in another and drugs criminals in another. They also kept all the young offenders banged up together, creating a breeding ground for Scotland's gangs of the future.

I feared who I'd be sharing a cell with. If you were assigned the wrong cellmate, your time became an unescapable hellhole, where you dared not sleep in case they tried to bugger or kill you. With a stroke of luck, they put me in a cell with Mickey from Fife. An ex-amateur boxer, he was inside for giving his wife a good hiding, or so he told me. We stayed up most nights chatting about boxing: what fighter was doing what, dissecting fights, analysing fighters, who we'd met over the years, etc. It was a good distraction. In here, I was fortunate to be a diehard pugilist, if only mentally, and have someone to talk boxing with. It was a much-needed escape from my situation.

While in jail, I just needed to keep my head down, look sharp and avoid eye contact at all times, unless I wanted to get cut. People had weapons, mostly sharpened knives stolen from the canteen or shanks made from bits of metal lifted from the workshops. There were also lots of drugs. The prison officers were either blind to it or didn't care.

Me and Mickey were sitting in the recreational area, watching football on telly, when a big geezer with crack-smoking brown teeth piped up and interrupted the match.

'Hey, you!' I always ignored conversations that started like that, unless I knew they were directed at me. 'Hey … pikey!' And these were.

'Cork it, fat boy,' I said in a voice that filled the room.

'Where d'ya get your fancy shoes, pikey?'

I was wearing regulation, slip-on black Borstals, which didn't match with my B&Q orange-coloured tracksuit.

He turned to his pals, who surrounded him, and started laughing. Like hyenas, they joined the chorus. I didn't want to nail this cunt because I didn't want to stay in jail longer. I would put him and his pals in hospital. I was sitting next to my cellmate, who, by all accounts, was pretty handy with his fists.

'I got them from someplace you haven't robbed yet, you junky bastard. You want a kick in your shit-stained teeth?' Surprisingly, he sat down and didn't make a bother. I should've been a politician. But to stop a fire, just don't light a match. Eventually my lawyer, Ian Scott, came to see me. It was the first visit I'd had from anyone.

'You've taken your fucking time but it's good to see you. I've had enough of this fucking place. Let's get me out of here.'

'What have you done, Scott? Room's not wired, so spout it out.'

'Nothing, I swear. Fuck all. On the Bible.'

'This is a big thing. In my opinion, you won't get bail and they want to extradite you to Malta to stand trial.'

'There is not a scrap of evidence against me. Someone just accused me but I'm fucking innocent.'

'If you say so, Scott. But you could still spend a year here while we try to prove that. Going back to Malta may be a better idea. It'll happen anyway but agreeing to the extradition now may be the lesser of two evils. You know what this place is like.'

'Don't they need evidence to extradite me? Surely, they do. Look, I'm no lawyer but isn't that the case?'

'My advice is to go back to Malta and clear your name. It could take forever to do that from here.'

'Clearing my name *will not* be straightforward in Malta. It's the dark side of the moon where law is concerned. Trust me.'

I hesitated to sign the extradition order but decided to take my lawyer's advice. At the time, I figured nothing could be much worse than my present situation. I prayed that when I explained where I was, on the day that Sammut got nicked for the dope, I'd be cleared of the charges and that would be that. Catching a break would be a fine thing for once in my life. But Malta was definitely Malta, and things were different there.

After five weeks in Edinburgh jail, I was handcuffed and put on a plane to Heathrow, then driven to Gatwick. After sitting in a holding cell for two hours, I was officially handed over to two special assignment Maltese officers, who had flown over to escort me. I knew both guys on a first-name basis. Malta was like a village, where everyone knew everyone. I had trained one of the guys at my gym and we had got on pretty good. They handcuffed me and took me through the departure lounge, where photographers were snapping photos of me. We went straight through the passport control area and they marched me to the plane with armed-response cops following in our wake. To me, it all seemed a bit over the top and totally unnecessary.

Next thing, I was sandwiched in between the two of them. The Malta flight was packed full of holidaymakers and kids. Most passengers couldn't have failed to notice that

I was handcuffed. With my hands tied, I tried to eat a packet of peanuts. Tied and busting was no way to fly and I'd never make it to Malta without going to the toilet. Air Malta didn't offer movies or music, so there was nothing else to do but talk to my captors.

'This is a big deal, Scott. Half a ton of grass? It's all over the papers and Sammut is pinning the whole thing on you. He said he was working for you and all the dope was yours,' said Marco, the SAG member I'd trained.

'Get real, Marco, will you? I had nothing to do with it. Sammut stitched me up and you lot believe him. I wasn't even on the island. If all that stuff was mine, do you honestly think I would've left?'

'Maybe it would be a good reason to,' replied Marco.

Whatever I said, the Maltese cops seemed pretty well convinced I was behind the biggest drug swoop in the island's history, like I was Al Capone or something. After we landed, we sat for 20 minutes until everyone, including the crew, emptied the plane. Malta's chief inspector of the drugs squad was standing at the bottom of the stairway. 'Welcome home, Scott. We've been waiting for you,' he said. I was pushed into the back of an old Skoda police car, driven to the Floriana police headquarters and quickly escorted to an interview room, where the chief inspector sat at a wooden table.

'Well, Mr Dixon, how was your flight?' he asked.

'Could've been better. Wish the bar was open.' He chuckled then frowned.

'One of my officers will be interviewing you soon.'

'Good. I can't wait to get this whole mess cleared up.'

About an hour later, an officer I didn't know came in and sat down. 'You've taken your time. How can I help you?' I asked. He wasn't amused that I was calm and collected, but I hadn't done anything wrong.

'Mr Dixon, can you tell me why you're here?'

'No sir, I honestly can't. I've read the charges and on the date of the incident, I was in Milan representing Malta, as you know. This whole situation is tarnishing my reputation. I have a gym to run and I should sue the pants off you.' He just started laughing. 'You may think this is funny, but I don't. In fact, the combination of you lot here and that lot in Scotland have inconvenienced me more than words can describe.'

'Enough. Are you ready to make a statement?'

'A statement about what? And where's my lawyer?'

'You're in Malta, my friend. We can hold you for 48 hours before we allow a lawyer anywhere near you. During that time, no phone calls either. For the time being, you belong to us.' Guilty until proven innocent was Maltese justice, it seemed, completely arse-about-face.

'Then I have nothing to say for 48 hours. I've been here for two hours already, so let's call it 46 hours, shall we?'

'We *will* talk to you later, count on it.'

They took me downstairs and shoved me into a stinking cell, packed with the great unwashed, like something out of *Midnight Express*. It was that bad. Six Libyans were lying on piss-stained mattresses and the rest of the space was filled with an amalgam of Africans and Maltese. In the corner, a plastic bucket was brimming with urine. Armies of ants marched across the walls, and cockroaches were everywhere. It must've been 100°F, with enough humidity to soak you right through the skin. I found a space on the floor as far away from the piss bucket as possible and sat down in the corner. One more slash and it would overflow. I figured the best thing for me to do was keep my mouth shut, ride the storm and hope it blew over. Hope was all I had.

I was drifting off to sleep when a loud voice woke me.

'Dixon, you're coming with us. Get up.' I was forcibly pushed all the way to the interview room. The same officer I'd talked to earlier was there, along with a fat, ugly brute of a guy, like *Shrek*, standing next to him. The room had no windows, so the air was thick and rancid. Cigarette smoke hung like filthy, acrid clouds, while the ashtrays overflowed with smouldering fag ends and ash.

'Right, Mr Dixon, let me ask you again. Do you have something to tell us?'

'Let me tell you again. Not one word from me until my lawyer is here.'

'You're a boxer with a name, Scott, so just tell us what we want to know, then we'll try to help you with the situation.'

'I have nothing to say.' He just leaned back in the chair and told the officers to take me back to the cell.

'We're not finished with you, Scott. We haven't even started,' he said as I left the room.

Every two hours, they put me through the same routine. I was manhandled back to the interrogation room, where they asked the same questions, then I'd give the same answers. Every time I was nearly asleep, it seemed, they'd drag me back for more and so it went on. They began denying me food and water and, like something out of the movies, started shining an angle-poise lamp in my face. Acting like first-year Gestapo trainees in short, brown trousers, they threatened me with all kinds of things. After three days, they moved me to the Corradino Correctional Facility, which was supposed to be a prison, but compared to Edinburgh, it was like Disneyland. Corradino's actual motto was 'firm but gentle', while Edinburgh's motto wasn't 'you're fucked' but should be.

My lawyer was waiting for me in a private room, just a tiny space with one door and no window. Finally, I was alone with someone I hoped could sort out this mess. If I had actually been guilty, it would've been one thing, but I was innocent and my patience was wearing thin. I also started regretting signing the extradition order.

'Sorry I couldn't see you until now. I tried more times than I can tell you. How was your time at police headquarters? Any complaints other than the conditions?'

'It's not the Hilton.'

'Anything physical? Beatings, torture, drugs? No polygraph, I imagine. They have it but don't know how to use it. They'd just make up the results. We may need one of those done in the future, but everything will have to be imported. We'd need our own machine and polygrapher but that whole process would be expensive. Let's just hope it doesn't come to that.'

'Nothing brutal. Just exhausted. They asked me the same fucking questions again and again, and I kept telling them I had nothing to do with it. Cloth ears and soft brains, I guess. So, what's happening? Why exactly am I here?'

'Kevin Sammut was caught with 500 kilos of marijuana. He says it was yours and that you employed him. He probably chose you because you've been seen together. You know how small the island is. You're also a foreigner, so he figured you'd be an easy target.'

I told my lawyer my side of the story: Sammut had only asked me to be muscle a few times when he cruised the bars and strip clubs, so yes, we would've been seen together. The 24-carat shitbag paid me to protect him and that was all. The real problem was two-fold: the 500 kilos of Rastafarian Old Holborn was a ton of smoke, and the authorities were notorious for believing what they wanted to believe. This wasn't even mentioning the Maltese mafia.

'So, how do I get out of here? What happens next? What am I going to do?'

'I apply for bail. It won't be easy and could be costly. But trials like this can be a very lengthy procedure.'

He also told me something I found hard to believe. Sammut had been in custody for a week. He was guilty. He was caught with the stuff but after a week he was out on bail. Between Scotland and Malta, I'd been locked up for nearly two months. There was no justice in it. I figured Sammut had friends in high places. So far, I'd been arrested, extradited, embarrassed and interrogated, and a pretty horny

Jacqueline had been dragged out of bed and dumped on the floor. Something smelled very wrong and fishy about all of it.

I reckoned the Maltese government was embarrassed about the big drug bust, even though they had nailed it. They probably wanted to now send a message to the holidaymakers with a conviction. Not that Malta was a drug island. Of course, it was! Show me an island that isn't. I always figured the government was coining it. The toe-rags wanted it every which way. Drugs were here, like everywhere, and that's what pulled in so many young people. I could've actually used some of Sammut's puff right now.

My lawyer left, and I was taken into the prison. On the surface, it looked alright. The inmates were walking around, and people were playing cards and dominoes. Army would've liked it.

'This looks okay,' I said to one of the guards who looked familiar.

'Okay for them, not for you. You're going to Division Six, maximum security. A word of warning, Scott. There's a big Arab serial killer in there, who's been real trouble to other inmates. Be advised to steer well clear of him.'

Division Six was divided into two tiers with 20 inmates in each area. The upper level was meshed, so you couldn't chuck yourself off on to the stone floor below. I was on the bottom deck in cell five. It had one barred window but was too high to look out of. The old gallows were still in the courtyard, where hundreds were hanged over the centuries, the last being a Protestant like me, but the courtyard was now a recreation area.

When I walked in with the screws, the conversations seemed to stop and everyone stared. I sat down at a table alone and a guy who looked familiar got up from the next table and joined me.

'Scott, there's a big Arab in here. We call him Gatto. You're new, so he'll come and make demands on you.'

'Yeah, I've heard this story. Let him fucking try.'

'Okay, but at least you know. He sits in his cell most of the time during the day, but when he comes out, he's brutal.'

'Yeah, thanks man. I've got the picture.'

'He's lost it. He cuts himself with a razor all day, then turns it on us.'

'Not me, pal. Watch and see.'

'Hey, he's already coming,' he whispered. Ten seconds later, I felt a hand on my shoulder.

'Give me your tobacco,' he growled. I ignored him. He shook my shoulder.

'Give me your fucking tobacco,' he shouted.

'What?'

'Give it now!' I rose from my chair, turned around and faced him. His face, neck and arms bore long thin scars all over, some of them criss-crossed, others like lines to play noughts and crosses on. 'Okay. It's in my cell, let's go,' I said.

He followed me into my cell, where my cellmate was sitting on his bunk reading the paper. His face dropped. I spun around and hit Gatto with a right uppercut followed by a sweet left. He headed for the stone floor. I got my cellmate to help me drag the big lump out of our cell, and we dumped him on the floor. He was out cold for ten minutes. He never bothered me again and the screws never once mentioned it.

During the day, everyone mixed because there was no segregation. Young offenders, nonces, drug traffickers, serial killers and rapists were all in one big pot of stew – the really bad and not so bad. I eventually got pally with Joey, who I'd just brand as an opportunist. He was inside for robbing churches disguised as a priest on Gozo Island.

One day, Joey went into the priest's quarters, halfway through a service, to find silver goblets and wads of cash. He then spotted a bishop's outfit, including the mitre. So, he put it on and walked out with a holdall, only to bump straight into a cop standing outside. The cop noticed he was wearing Nike trainers, sporting a flash Rolex and had tattoos on his hands – not exactly styled like your average bishop. Compared to the rest of Malta's law enforcement, that cop in Gozo should've been made chief of police just for his powers of observation. Johnny was sentenced to seven years.

While at Corradino, my strategy was simple: make it as easy as possible for myself by making nice with the guards. I showed an interest in them, asking questions about their families, looking at phone photos of their kids, etc. After some time, it worked. Bit by bit, they gave me privileges that other inmates didn't have. While other inmates were locked down from 12pm to 2pm, then 8pm to 6am, my cell door stayed unlocked day and night. I also spent a lot of time in the prison gym. I'd work out and train the guards, which was an okay way to pass the time and better than sitting around doing nothing. But I never forgot that I could be facing endless years of this shit.

Repeated bail requests fell on deaf ears. I was rejected 29 times before I was granting a hearing. But on that occasion, the court proceedings were a fucking shambles. My brief was stuttering like a schoolboy on his first date, and the judge kept interrupting him, so I figured I didn't have a chance. But a pal, who owns nightclubs, put up €19,000 and my mum signed a personal guarantee for another €25,000. The bail conditions were tight with a very strict curfew. I couldn't leave the apartment between 11pm and 7am. I also had to sign in and out at the police station twice daily or it was straight back inside. I couldn't leave the St Julian's area or go on the water. So, it was like being in an outdoor prison, which was a hell of a lot better than being inside a real one.

With the strict restraints, I decided to put all of my energy back into professional boxing but every time I applied for a boxing licence, I was rejected because of my pending court case, which amounted to unfinished business. That's how it was seen. So, I began boxing unlicenced in Malta, much to Papa's disapproval. I had 16 fights, with 16 wins and seven knockouts. I started betting on myself and even pocketed a few thousand euros. Then, out the blue, I received a Facebook message from Torsten Knille.

'Hey champ, I used to love watching you fight. You're a great fighter. Why aren't you boxing pro anymore?

Guess what?! I'm the new president of the WBU. Keep in touch.'

'I can't get a licence,' I messaged back.

'Apply for a German licence,' he responded.

So, I did just that and got my licence. I went in for the scans, passed all the fitness tests and was pronounced in A-1 condition. So, I began looking for a warm-up fight with just about anybody from any place who fancied it. After not too long – and I could hardly believe it, considering everything – I surprisingly got offered a shot at the world title.

Round 10

Rehab

January 2012

As the church bells rang, and fireworks painted the Maltese sky to welcome in the new year, I made one resolution to do something about me. The Christmas holiday hadn't been easy for me or anyone who knew me. I had been fractious, jumpy, rude and a total pain in the arse, so much so that I could see the frustration and worry in other people's eyes.

I couldn't be in any specific room, or in any specific place, for more than five minutes. Everybody tried to be nice and calm me down, but I was very ill at ease in my own skin. I felt like I had been back in Hairmyres Hospital in Hamilton, when I was coming off morphine. Only this time, I was on pretty much everything else and out of control. There was no denying that.

My mum said I was an alcoholic and drug addict – without direction or ambition – and was becoming a disgrace and disappointment to everyone, especially Papa, who'd stuck by me through thick and thin all my life. Maybe 'disgrace' was the word that got me to stop and think. I went to see my boxing doctor, who was also our family doctor and friend, Mark Xuereb. I spilled my heart out to him, leaving nothing out. Well, almost nothing. Mark knew me well, so a lot of it was old news. Only now, I was actually saying it and not just showing it.

He told me about a new psychiatric unit he could get me into, where I could detox if necessary. I would have proper evaluations and counselling but had to stay for four weeks.

'You might as well know in advance, Scott. It's not a holiday camp. It's an actual asylum, but you might get the chance to see how crazy you are or you're not ... You're giving me a strange look. What are you thinking?'

'I've seen the film. Do you guarantee I won't get a lobotomy like Jack Nicholson?'

He smiled.

I wasn't doing anything else, so on 20 January I checked myself in. Mark didn't think I was crazy, but I was hardly balanced or normal. I was paranoid, jealous and full of rage and envy. Serious depression had also got hold of me again and wouldn't let go. Alcohol and cocaine brought all of this to a head and something had to give.

I drove myself to the cuckoo's nest and sat in the car for ten minutes before going in. I closed my eyes and asked God to help me. 'Dear God, please show me the way ...' I had no problem handing myself over to a Higher Power. I had always been a believer anyway. But, handing myself over to psychiatric nurses, who I'd never go with, and a bunch of shrinks who talked in riddles wasn't so easy.

During the first few days, I was on detox medication, so I was either asleep or awake with a head without a brain. I didn't crave anything; the drugs saw to that. Bit by bit, as the drugs loosened their grip, I think they started to replace my meds with placebos. At the same time, I couldn't tell them from proper medication because I had no fucking idea what was going on.

After a week, a fella in a white coat, no stethoscope, came to see me and asked me to write my life story. What? This wasn't a proper psychiatric hospital, it must be Enid Blyton's cottage in the Lake District that Grandma used to tell me about. When I got my bunny Snowy, she'd suggested the name Peter. But, as I'm here, I might as well give it a crack.

As one half of me started writing, the other half of me couldn't believe what I was scribbling down. My pen was moving but my eyes couldn't take it in. What a fucking mess; who am I? The more I wrote, the more disconnected from the story I felt. Maybe I should do the decent thing, like Billy, and put everyone else out of their misery in one fell swoop.

Every other day, I had a one-to-one with the head nutcracker, Doctor Amusse. He was a family man, by the looks of it, with framed photographs of a woman and children. On one of his shelves, he had framed certificates to prove he was a *bona fide* psychiatrist and not a patient masquerading as a quack. 'Anything's possible,' my grandfather always used to tell me.

These one-to-one, face-to-face sessions were round-for-round brutal, revealing and difficult.

'I want you to write a list of all the people you've damaged the most, and we'll go through it next time,' he said at the end of our first session. Two days later, I handed him a sheet of paper. He looked at it and then handed it back to me, offering me a pen at the same time.

'You've missed someone off.'

'Who?'

'You. Put your name on the list.' I wrote my name at the bottom of the page and handed the piece of paper back to him. He drew a circle around my name, drew a line to the top of the page and put an arrow next to it.

'The person you have damaged the most is you. If I can't find a way to help you like yourself, ideally love yourself, there's no hope, Scott.' This guy was worth every one of those letters after his name. I wanted to cry but I didn't. Jesus, I needed to cry and let it all out. I was about to burst.

'I'd never thought about it like that before.'

'Most people don't. What do you want to be?'

'World champion.'

'Is that all?'

After the session, I walked slowly back to my room, went in and closed the door. I threw myself on to the bed, laid back, stared at the ceiling and began to cry like a baby. When I woke up in the morning, with my day clothes still on, my pillow was soaked wet through. At least I had started to let it out. Even in my sleep.

I sensed my doctor had another viewpoint on me. I felt like someone else was talking to him. At this point, nobody came to see me except Gary, my manager and business partner, who visited every day. Maybe Doctor Amusse had collared him to help fill in the gaps that I couldn't remember or didn't want to. But, I knew Gary would only spout if he thought it might help. He's as good as family blood. Maybe he'd been part of this whole intervention, when people only want you to recover.

The people who actually care about you most only want to make some sense of you when you're senseless. One day, Gary came to see me and explained to me what I had suspected.

'Just so you know, and hear it from me, I wanted to help you with your recovery in any way I could, so I had a private chat with your doctor.'

'Yeah?'

'Just to tell him what you might not have told him.'

'Such as?'

'That people are terrified of you.'

'Are you?'

'No.'

'What else did you say, other than talk about Everton? You and Amusse have that in common, if nothing else.'

'Basically, that you are dangerous and can clear a packed bar in a minute just by walking in. But, I don't think you've recovered from the attack. You feel betrayed. We talked about Papa, too. He said that your desire to be like him is a stumbling block because you aren't like him. You'd like to be, but aren't, and probably never will be.' I thought about what I was hearing. Gary leaned in and kept on.

'And that your obsession with Jesus is fine to a point but it's grown extreme.'

'What did he say to that?'

'He asked me if I had ever heard of Bible John from Glasgow.'

'Who?'

'No idea. Some fucking Scottish nutcase, obviously. He also said that whilst you are not in prison, you are contained in Malta, on a curfew, and restricted to St Julian's. He said that sooner or later, when anyone's freedom is limited, there will be a breakout, a rebellion. He's worried about that.'

In between seeing the doctor, as well as having a lot of time to think and try to tune my mind, I also had a lot of time to train. Nothing too strenuous; push ups, squats, all those basic exercises. I asked for a skipping rope but was denied in case I used it to hang myself or strangle a patient. There were a few in the nuthouse who would've thanked me in the afterlife for doing it.

During the next session with Amusse, I asked him how he thought I was doing.

'When you came here I saw a man whose eyes told me he wanted to die. I'm beginning to see a man who wants to live, so it's so far so good. It's not an easy road to travel, Scott. Many fall by the wayside and return to what's familiar, because what is unfamiliar is too challenging.'

I did want to live. Two weeks from now, I'm thinking I would look for a job as a minister – maybe even as a father. When I was in detox before, people use to say, 'It will get better.' My diagnosis before was straightforward. I had abused alcohol and drugs but wasn't considered an addict who had no power over it. Maybe. I wasn't too sure about that, either, because I'd binge drink, then take a day or two off, then binge again.

But, according to the doctor now, my problem wasn't the drugs and alcohol. I was heavily entrenched in post-traumatic stress following the attack, which had taken root and caused the severe depression. If I had been attacked by complete strangers, would it have been less traumatic? I'll never know. But it wasn't all psychobabble in there. There were recreational arts and crafts hobby classes. Gary and now my mum were allowed to visit me but no one else. They were searched each time to make sure they hadn't brought me anything. One day, I made a basket and gave it to Gary.

'Well, I've seen everything now,' he laughed. 'A basket from a basket-case. I'll cherish this, pal.'

There were some proper basket-cases in there, though. Big fat Rocco was just one of many. I was in the cafeteria having dinner one evening and sitting opposite Rocco. He'd come to join me because I couldn't stomach the food and said so. So, Rocco would sit next to me when he could. I was a free meal. One day like many, he watched me play with my food, shoving it this way and that, trying to find even a pea I wanted to eat. I pushed my plate towards him. Rocco pulled the plate closer to him, stared at it for a moment and then tucked in without a word, like a starving man who hadn't eaten for a week.

After spreading half a packet of butter on a bread roll, he suddenly leant right down on to the plate to shovel mashed potato into his face. When he lifted his head up, the bread roll was stuck to his forehead. He was looking everywhere for it. I'd not had a laugh in there until then but now I was literally trying not to piss myself. A nurse came over, gave me a tut-tut and unglued the bread roll from Rocco's forehead and handed it to him. She wiped his forehead clean and gave me the daggers.

'You shouldn't laugh. That could be you, Dixon. Make no mistake about that.'

I had to leave the room. I went out of the door and stood in the corridor. It took me a good 15 minutes before the laughter subsided. I wasn't sure if my tears were of laughter or something a lot less funny. Being there was a leveller, one way or another, and you had a lot of time to think. I didn't want to be stuck in there forever, like a lot who would be. I'd have to muster up the strength to chuck a massive fridge through a barred window, take off for the hills and hope like hell I could make it to somewhere where I could lie down and rest.

I had my own room, but it wasn't private. The door was always open, so the night duty staff could come around with flashlights and check that everyone was alright, alive and accounted for. One night, I was woken by the sound of someone in my room. I flicked on my light and a guy was standing over me but looked asleep.

'Wake up,' I said loudly. He opened his eyes and made two fists.

'What are you doing in my room?' he yelled.

'It's my room, you moron. Fuck off.'

He stared at me with glazed eyes as saliva dribbled down his chin. I'd had enough of this. I wanted out on any terms and conditions. I pressed my alarm button. The alternative was to deck him, but I didn't want to do that. In seconds, two night-staff guys came in and took hold of him by the arms and led him away. He was insisting there was someone in his room.

'Put a lock on my fucking door, will you? If any of your lunatics do that again to me, you'll be responsible,' I shouted after them. Unable to sleep, I laid awake all night, wired. I ain't doing this again, ever. Not for me, my doctor, nobody.

Amusse let me out after 18 days. He thought there had been what he called 'an improvement'. No way was I ever going back there again. Whatever my doctor had hoped to achieve had worked all right. Being in that asylum was definitely a once-in-a-lifetime experience for me. Thank God it wasn't the full four weeks or even longer.

After my discharge, I devoted all of my energy to the fight that had been set up before detox. It was time to get my arse into gear. I put down the booze and fags, kept my nose clean and set about a ten-week intensive training camp at the gym. For once, the curfew was a blessing in disguise. Training was ten weeks of early nights and eight hours' sleep. Most of the time, I did my roadwork and trained alone. I had no coach to push me but drove myself hard. I'd hit the punch bag for half an hour without stopping, followed by 200 press-ups, then 1,000 skips with the rope, alternating feet.

I studied my opponent's fights, looking for weak spots and checking his endurance. He could hit alright and my mind replayed my fight career. Where had I gone wrong when I lost? When was I not razor-sharp? I needed to be more match-fit now, more so than any previous time in my life, but I was definitely big-fight ring rusty.

Two weeks into my training, my pal Demis asked me to help him out at a boxing show in Bugibba. I applied for a curfew extension, which was always a hassle with all the palaver attached. I did get authorised permission to leave St Julian's but had to be back home no later than 2.30am. One night, I got home at 2.28am, right in the nick of time.

Next morning, someone had their finger glued to my intercom buzzer. I answered and was handed a letter by a man who looked like he didn't want to be there. He told me I had breached my bail conditions and had to appear in court at 2pm that day. It was just another irritation, a cheap shot at me. The only way through all the bollocks was to toe the line and turn up. But, ultimately, I needed to prove my innocence, so these morons would lay off me and let me live my life.

One of the inspectors went to see Frankie, the club owner who had put up the €19,000 for my initial bail. The inspector told Frank that I'd breached my bail conditions. Hardly surprisingly, Frankie withdrew the bail money, so fuck. I went to court armed with a receipt from the taxi guy, who'd written down the time he dropped me off. It didn't wash with the court, so I was back inside and my training programme had gone all to cock.

My new manager, Gary Hincks, wanted to sign as a guarantor but they wouldn't let him because he was English. So, Gary flew back to England, got the cash and got me out of jail. 'A friend in need ...' While he was gone, some traitor in my camp contacted the WBU and tried to get the fight called off. And Gary said he had been threatened. I knew who the saboteur was but needed to stay focused.

I first met Gary Hincks in 2010 at Tony's Bar on the harbour front. It was the type of place where local men came in first thing in the morning for a coffee and a smoke, read the newspaper and watched tourists pass in tight shorts and tighter tops. Some stayed for hours. It was better than going home. It's a man's place where boys talked boy stuff, and everyone grumbled about their wives and children and nothing. I was in Tony's having a coffee when I heard this big fella, who I'd never seen before, talking to two men with thick Liverpudlian accents. Nothing attracts a Scottish bloke like that voice. It's like a magnet.

He was a stranger and I'm wary of strangers. You never know who's after you. He kept looking at me, so I crossed the road and sat down on a bench and waited for them to leave. When they finally left, I went back into Tony's and asked the manager who they were.

'No idea, Scott. They're new to the island as far as I know. They've been coming here for the last three days.'

Next day, they were there again. I went over to the big fella and asked him if he'd finished with his newspaper. 'Yeah, mate, it's all yours,' he said in a thick Liverpool accent. I sat down at the table next to them and listened to them talk. All three of them were Scousers, sounding like John Lennon in full flow. I was cat jumpy. I went across the road to McDonald's, where they had an upstairs balcony. It was a perfect site for me to watch them. They left, then came back three hours later. They sat outside, had something to eat, left again and then came back an hour later. What was going on? They had all the outward appearances of a hit squad. This carried on for four days. I needed to get to the bottom of it and finally leave McDonald's.

One day, the big guy was wearing an Everton shirt. That was as good a chance as any to engage him in conversation. 'Hello, mate, your team are doing pretty good at the moment.'

'Yeah, not bad, who are you?' he asked. We had a chat. All went fine. No trouble, no need. Pity he wasn't Scottish but nobody's perfect. That was the ice breaker. All that shit in my head was just paranoia. I must've been expecting something, maybe from Scotland or maybe from Malta. Regardless, Big Gary and I hit it off large.

Gary's a funny Scouser with a quick wit. What he lacked in height, he made up for in width. He was a wide boy in the best physical sense of the word, not one of those Cockneys. He landed on the island because he got fed up with Liverpool. He owned pubs and clubs there, but some stuff must've gone down. I didn't pry too hard into his story.

We knocked about together and stayed up all night. He had opened a restaurant called Meet Steakhouse, now owned a few nightclubs and drove a bright yellow Jeep, which he would lend me. When you saw me, you'd see Gary and vice versa, so we decided to start working together. I could fight and do things he couldn't. He could fix, organise and do other things I couldn't. Gary, when he got out of bed, made things happen. A wily sort, he also had some cash and connections. In Malta, you don't own restaurants or clubs, even a golf club membership or mooring for a boat, without knowing what makes the island tick.

As good as things were going with Gary at the time, he started coming to the gym about the same time 'trouble' came into my life. She was a TV presenter, singer and a terrible flirt. I was giving her private, one-on-one physical training workouts, when she made it crystal-clear she'd got the hots for me.

'I have fallen in love with you,' she whispered in my ear after one of our workouts. Next thing, we're on the toilet doing the business. When we opened the door, Gary was standing there grinning.

'That sounds like a good one-to-one. Don't forget to flush.'

The next evening, when she turned up for training, she showed me a tattoo saying 'Dixon's Property' on the inside of her arm. Jesus, 'kiss and tell' had turned into 'show and tell'. This was now 'trouble' in stereo. I knew her fella was going to go nuts. I whistled Gary over to take a look.

'She's a fucking bunny boiler,' he mumbled under his breath as he walked away.

Out of the blue, I was summoned to court to have my bail conditions reviewed. The inspector in charge of my case read out a string of offences where I had failed to sign in or had been seen and photographed in the early hours of the morning. I was now confined to the St Julian's boundary, not much better than an open prison, with no means of earning. I couldn't get to my gym, so that went tits up. I was stuffed.

A week later, I got a call from a boxer I used to train. 'I need to talk to you but not on the phone.'

'Okay, when?'

'Today.'

He'd been training a big Polish guy who'd asked if he knew me. He said he did and we were friends. Apparently, the Polish guy was offered €100,000 to kill me, half up front and the rest on completion. Although he said he refused the offer, the would-be hitman still wanted to meet me. I thought about that. Weigh-in stares are important.

'Okay, tell him five o'clock at Gary's restaurant. I need to know what's going on.'

The restaurant was empty, and the street was quiet. Me and Gary had a pint and waited. We heard footsteps coming up the stairs. In walked a 6ft 8in guy with a millimetre of blonde hair. He was a massive fucker you could spot a mile off. I noticed his left index 'trigger' finger was missing. Obviously, he was right-handed. When he sat down to join us, the chair creaked with the weight of 16 or 17 stones plonking on it. Without hesitation or niceties, he put a few pieces of paper on the table.

'Here. Someone wants you dead. Take a look.' He produced copies of four emails back and forth as proof, a rundown contract of my hit.

'Why are you doing this?' I asked him.

'It smelt wrong. We're fighters and I know you.' He smiled a bit and leaned back. 'But don't you ever fuck with my sister, or I'll do it for nothing.' He looked like Army, only bigger. Think Klitschko. I wouldn't want to be in the ring with him; I'd be face down in seconds.

I thanked him, and the Polish giant left. I went straight to the police station, only two doors away, holding the four copies of the emails. The next day, three people were arrested. But it wasn't all doom and gloom. Actually, me and Gary had some good laughs about it all.

I wasn't allowed on the water but never took much notice of that. One day, Gary and I were on a shit-hot fast, 250-horsepower Kawasaki jet ski capable of 69 knots. We were doing tight circles smashed out of our skulls, and I hung to him like a motorbike tart going on honeymoon. The jet ski flipped over about 500 metres from the shore and we couldn't right it.

'Swim for the shore. We'll make a phone call and get the cunt that lent us this fucking thing to get his arse over here in a boat,' said Gary, bobbing up and down and spitting out seawater like a whale. He always made me laugh and never more than on that occasion.

'I've got €3,000 under the seat and I'm not fucking leaving here without it,' said Gary, gasping for air.

'Gary, is that a shark or what?' I asked, imitating his accent. His face dropped, his eyes opened to full and he looked all around him.

'Fuck off, you twat.'

I'm not the fastest swimmer on earth and the breaststroke is all I'm good at. So, it took a while before I dragged myself on to one of the few bits of sand on this God-forsaken rock of an island I couldn't leave.

When I got to shore, I wasn't alone. There must have been about 500 people at a society wedding. It was in full swing and packed with complete swankers. I unzipped the top of my wetsuit, pulled out my mobile and made the call. Twenty-five minutes later, Gary came out of the water, like Ursula Andress, only a million times less fuckable. He had seaweed stuck to his legs and snot dribbling out of his nose. Not a pretty sight. How he ever persuaded anyone to marry him was a mystery.

He collapsed on the sand next to me, and we started giggling like two deranged kids who'd seen a pair of tits through a keyhole. As we were there, we decided to join the party. It was full of 'Malteasers'. Anybody who was anybody, and a lot who wished they were, were all dolled up to the nines, rubbing shoulders and making chit-chat about bugger all. The biggest, fully staffed bar I'd ever seen beckoned me like a call girl – a free call girl.

'Are you the entertainment?' asked a man in a turban. He was sporting a black silk bow tie and looked a bit twitchy.

'If you like, what would you like me to sing?' said Gary, his eyes making for the bar before his large body could follow.

People were giving us sideways looks, but eyes were mostly fixed on the family assembled for a wedding photograph. The photographer had finally got them where he wanted them. Even the kids had glued-on smiles when Gary popped up, next to the bride's father, waving a bottle of beer like a flag, giving the thumbs-up and grinning like a chimpanzee. He stayed there while the photographer shot off a roll of film. Click, click, click – Gary was in the wedding album.

'Which side of the family is he on? Can't be ours surely,' asked an old lady wearing a crimson hat with a bowl of fruit on it.

One of the guests kindly said he'd go and call us a taxi, but for some reason, a cop car turned up instead, so I was now in bother again with the authorities. The Maltese police totally lacked a sense of humour, like most of the Maltese. They're just a notch up from the Germans. Malta has been invaded, raped, pillaged, infiltrated, bombed and occupied so many times in its long history that the Maltese were like a beef and vegetable stew with 30 ingredients in it. It's a load of all sorts but with no flavour. The lack of humour could be from all the invading, raping, pillaging, infiltrating, bombing and occupying, but who knows?

I came out of prison carrying two big bin-liner bags full of clothes. Gary was waiting for me across the road in his yellow Jeep, grinning like a Cheshire cat. Either the bin bags were making him laugh, or he was off his head.

'Stop, don't move. I've got to capture this,' he said. He took a photo on his phone.

'This one's for the book you keep banging on about, if you ever get your arse into gear to write one, which I very much doubt. What you gonna call it then? "Fuckwit" would be my title,' he laughed.

Over time, it became clear that there was a definite conspiracy to stop the title fight in Malta. My training kept getting interrupted, and time was running out. I didn't know who was behind it or who to trust apart from Gary. But I had to believe one way or another, even if we had to grease palms, which was the accepted way to get anything done in Malta, that the fight would happen. Baker Barakat wasn't having to put up with shit like this. He'd be in Training Camp Perfect some place getting the best of the best: food, conditions, partners, equipment, advice, psychology and maybe even some tasty night comfort and encouragement. Me? Not much. Just suffocating weather and the law. Everything else was a tits-up shambles. The heat was the only blessing I could count on because I was used to it. Well, not the only blessing. Papa had seen fit to get on a plane to give me a hand with the challenge.

Not long ago, I had ten weeks to train, now I had six. I knew the seconds were ticking away at twice normal speed. While I was inside, my so-called business partner had been trying to replace me with Robin Reid, whose career started large after he won a bronze medal at the 1992 Olympics in Barcelona. But I called WBU president Torsten and explained what had happened, reassuring him that I was out of prison, and bingo! The fight was back on.

'You've six weeks. That's 42 days, Scott. So better get stuck in and good luck champ,' Torsten told me. He even sent us a piece of paper guaranteeing that it was a go. After the fight got straightened out, I rang the rat who had tried to get the fight called off and left a message. 'I'm out of prison. The fight is back on and if you want to come and meet me, I'm here.' I didn't hear a word back, so he was right out of the picture.

In prison, I was training two or three times a day with a couple of guys from Ghana. They were pretty good but static. But I'd got everyone to have a go. Even junkies were having a stab. Regardless, I was no way ready. Soon as I got out, me and the gang started training in an old, disused building. It was dusty with no windows and no ring, just two punch bags. Papa was there and was still a great trainer. Despite being 83 years old, he had come here with his heart. This was family, so this was serious business.

'It's hot as hell in here, son,' Papa said, walking into the gym. 'A lot stacked against you, but we'll make the best of this … it's not much, but we'll do.'

Papa spray-painted a black square on the floor, the exact size of a boxing ring. We sparred inside it. If I stepped over the line by an inch, he pulled me up. More than anything, I needed someone to give me pad work, someone to hold the big pads, move them side to side, up and down fast while I thumped them. In 2008, I'd boxed Ludvic Muscat at the most-attended fight in Maltese history, which was held in the basketball arena in Ta' Qali, but Muscat was long gone. He would've been my first pick for pad work. So, the only guy kicking around who might fit the bill was Steve Aquilina.

A half-Maltese, half-Brit raised in Birmingham, Aquilina was having a hard time making ends meet. In his heyday, Steve fought Chris Eubank in 1988 in Portsmouth. No spring chicken at 46, he was still tough as fuck. Nicknamed Cobra, which explained the Cobra tattoo on his head, Steve scared most people shitless. Along with so many others, he was a walking example of how boxing can ditch you after you've had your day.

Gary asked him how much he'd charge us for a workout. 'Give us €20, that'll do. Is that okay?' He turned up at our excuse for a gym looking like Huckleberry Finn, wearing frayed denim shorts, no shoes and just socks. This was my sparring partner. I started to think I had no chance. The image of the belt I had locked in my mind was starting to fade. I had an old pair of high-top basketball shoes hanging up on a rusty nail on the wall by the door. It was the best I could offer him.

'Hey, Steve, try these. They're better than nothing.' They fitted him and I could see he loved them.

'Hey, these are cool, Scott. Yeah, thanks man.' I could also see there was no way I'd ever get them back. He reached for a tatty plastic bag that was beyond recycling, pulled out a pair of welding gloves and put them on.

'Jesus, Steve, you can't wear those,' I said. 'Where the fuck did you find those things?'

'In a skip. Same place I found my socks.'

He'd got no bandages, gloves, gum shield, head guard, nothing. Although he'd more than done his time in the ring, he'd still be like a sitting duck. I would have been happier hammering a punch bag but had to give it a go.

'Look, Steve, I ain't gonna go easy on you. This is work time.'

'Don't worry, Scott, it'll be okay.'

First round, I was knocking him all over the place and not much was coming back. It wasn't right. Boiled eggs started popping up on his face. He stopped and turned to Gary, who was watching, stroking his chin and looking uncomfortable.

'I'm sliding around all over the place, like I'm on an ice rink,' Steve said. 'These shoes aren't built for the job. Take 'em off, Gary, will you?'

He sat down, and Gary dropped to his knees. I was watching Gary and knew what he was thinking. *Fuck this for a game of soldiers. I'm a manager, not a chiropodist.*

'Jesus Christ!' said Gary, trying not to hold his nose while ungluing his socks, which must've been on Steve's feet for two years. His long, gnarled toenails looked like they belonged on a lizard. If somebody had been filming this, nobody would've believed it. Preparation for a title fight? I fucking don't think so.

'I'll get you a footbath for Christmas, mate, and some carbolic soap and hot water,' said Gary, shaking his head. 'This is a fucking joke.'

The deal was four rounds for €20. After three rounds, he'd had enough. Steve looked like he'd just been hit by a motorbike and was sitting in the middle of road, dazed.

'Look mate, enough is enough, let's call it a day,' I said. I handed him €20. He reached for the boots while his eyes searched the room.

'Okay if I keep these? Where are my socks?' Gary looked at him and shook his head in disbelief.

'What the fuck, mate? Here's another €10. Buy some socks and nail clippers.'

We needed a good trainer 'el pronto' – like yesterday. We were on the back foot and if our rivals knew what was going on, they would've been laughing all the way to the bank.

Gary and I sat outside Julio's Bar on the harbour front. We drank water, which showed how bad things really were. While wondering what the hell we were going to do next, I spotted Ludwig stepping off a massive catamaran on to the top of the harbour wall. He's a trainer with a good record. Born with one silver spoon in his mouth and one up his arse, Ludwig was a Ferrari-driving playboy. He was a bit flash but also a good trainer.

Gary wolf-whistled. Ludwig spotted us and strolled over like he'd been taught how to walk in a rich, unhurried way. He sat down impeccably dressed. There wasn't a clothing crease in sight, even after a day at sea. His jet-black hair was slicked back, and he wore a permanent suntan. He was one of those people you'd never know what to buy for Christmas.

'Heya, Scott. You gonna win? Should I make a bet?' he asked.

Gary got straight to the point. The clock was ticking, and we needed someone immediately. 'Look sport, we need a trainer. Scott's going for a world title fight in a few weeks. You might like the challenge, too. There's not enough time for you to sleep on it, yes or no?' We'd pulled out all the stops while trying not to look *too* desperate. But we were more than desperate. It wasn't like Ludwig was on our shortlist. His was the only name on the page.

He smiled. He nodded. He laughed.

'Okay.' Game on.

'See you tomorrow at 9 o'clock, let's make sure we're all there.'

'What about payment?' I asked him.

'We can talk about that after you win.'

Ludwig was pure 24-carat gold, to my amazement and relief. He turned up bang on time with all the enthusiasm, spit and punch of a bloke who was going for the title himself.

He pushed me, and all of us, non-stop. I imagined he was doing this because he was bored out of his mind. With us, maybe he felt he was closer to being alive for a reason. It was a challenge for us all.

The first day on the pads, my timing was out. Everything he put up, I was missing. I'd become so used to working on lifeless dead weights that my speed skills were static, like I was moving in slow motion. He was as quick as light, I was slow and leaden. I was worried and doubting myself. Fortunately, he wasn't.

'Hey, don't worry, man. It will come back. We have time. See you tomorrow.'

He roared off in his red Ferrari, and I walked home deflated. I needed a reality check. Am I kidding myself? Is this a very bad joke? Am I on the slide? Have I slid?

Late that night, I got a Facebook message from someone who wasn't a Facebook friend. 'Are you still having nightmares about me?' It was from one of the guys who had tried to kill me in 2004. Fuck him. He's not worth the time. The next day, things began to shuffle back together just a little, but enough to spur me on and forget about yesterday. Yesterday was history. It was time to step up the pace.

I was sparring 14 rounds straight with four guys, alternating like a tag team, to keep the kettle boiling. Every weight and speed I could get. I'd fight small guys, who are quick but had nothing behind their punches, and big brutes that could easily drop you with one hit. Jap Kavanagh, my conditioning coach, pushed me further than I'd ever been before. He threw medicine balls at my body to see if I could deflect them or catch them. We fought with bare knuckles, which is a dividing line for anyone. You don't want to get caught, so bare knuckle sharpens you up like a knife. If you get cut, it shows, then one cut leads to another, always. And it's a target for any opponent.

The drop foot I had suffered from the attack had always plagued me, although with a lot of physio and special exercises over the years, it had got a little better. The physio helped keep my Achilles injury under control and reduce the swelling. However, a scan revealed I had a tear, just to make matters worse, so I couldn't run very far and had to use the bike instead. The doctors seemed dubious I would be able to fight.

I was at 79kg and needed to hit 76kg for the fight. I was burning weight but needed to keep most of it on. I'd eat four or five times a day: 600 grams of steak, 1,000 grams of chicken breast, big potatoes, vegetables and fruit – packing it in. Gary had a restaurant and the chef was instructed to give me whatever I needed. Gary footed the bill.

One week before the fight, I went to the gym, opened the door and stopped dead in my tracks. There was nothing in there. The punch bag, ceiling bag, skipping ropes, protectors and bikes were gone. Jesus! The front of the building was locked up like Fort Knox, so whoever had done this must have come in the back way, which would have been quite an ordeal, especially getting my stuff out of there. A punch bag takes some moving, especially down a ladder.

The robbery should've collapsed me, but I was so angry that it made me even more determined. No time to waste bothering about who'd done it, I just needed to keep cracking on. My ankle was still a serious issue. Last resort would be an anaesthetic injection but that can be very costly, and it can damage the Achilles even more. I was feeling the steel plate in my arm vibrating, too. An injection in the arm might also be necessary. Anaesthetics can interfere with the entire nervous system. In some cases, you can actually feel more pain in other parts of your body. Half of me was now wondering why the hell I was doing this fight at all. There's no way I would've put a bet on myself as things stood.

Federico Peltretti

Federico Peltretti

Federico Peltretti

Federico Peltretti

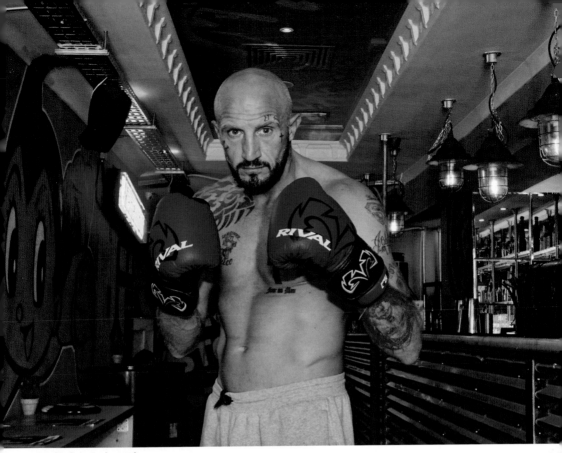

Federico Peltretti

Scott Dixon in front of the Lord's Gym in Malta **Federico Peltretti**

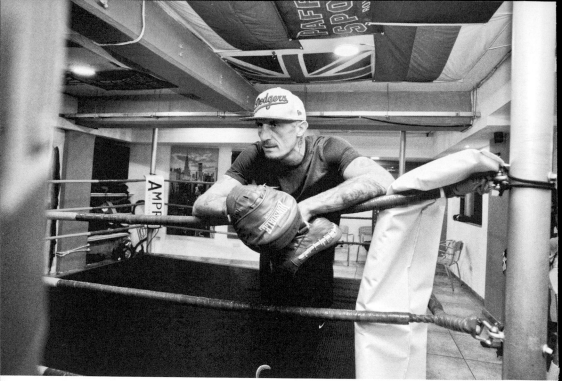

Federico Peltretti

Federico Peltretti

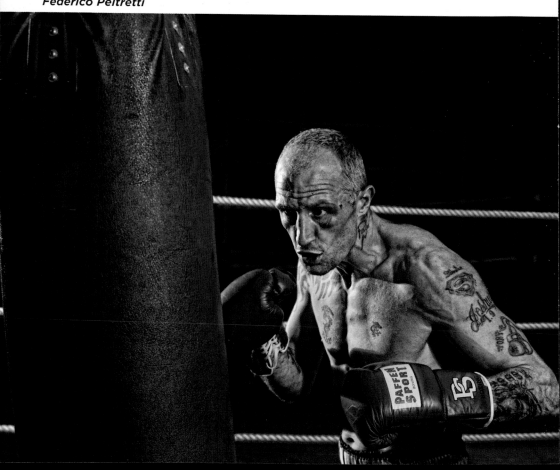

Papa and Scott Dixon
Federico Peltretti

Viktor Vella
Stills

Federico Peltretti

Viktor Vella Stills

(Left to right) Scott's father, Aunt Jennifer, Mum, Gran, Papa **Federico Peltretti**

Scott with son, Toby Dixon

2014 WBU super-middleweight defence against Georgi Kandelaki
Viktor Vella Stills

Round 11

Break!

August 2012. The day before the fight

I'd no time left before the fight. If I wasn't ready, one more
day of training wasn't going to make a scrap of difference. So,
I levelled with my camp. 'I'm not training today and taking
the day off. I'm as ready as I'll ever be body-wise, but my spirit
needs a shot of something.'

'You want steroids?' asked Emullo, half-laughing.

'No, I don't. I want something else. See you tomorrow.
My phone will be off.'

Nobody questioned or followed me. When I decided to do
something, I tried to make it pretty clear to everyone I meant
it. And a bit of mystery right now was no bad thing. Maybe
they thought I'd leave the island. Sell up, buy a yacht and set
sail around the world to find the meaning of life. I had seen
a movie with this guy who had a going-nowhere job in New
York City, and he did the same thing. He left a yellow Post-It
note on his office door with two words scribbled on it. GONE

FISHING. Toby was on my mind. He was now five years old, with a mop of blonde hair and innocent blue eyes. Do I get him a pair of boxing gloves? And if I do, will he end up like me, caught inside two worlds totally fucked. Like father, like son? I hoped not. Not for him, if I had anything to do with it. People play cricket, football, tennis, golf, but you don't play boxing. It's the hurt business with side effects. So, do I get him a cricket bat and an education? Do I nudge him into martial arts – maybe karate? Those black belt boys always had an unnerving air of calm around them, and they're not legally allowed to use the tricks of their trade, unless pushed to the limit. Trouble tends to evaporate because of their calm, assured attitude.

I'd worry about this stuff later. I decided to find a boat and take Toby off the island, just for a bit. Away from all the tourists who came here to get blasted and go home without a suntan. Malta catered to morons. Mum had a friend with a boat who said we could use it any time. I expected a small thing with an outboard motor and two fishing lines.

I was holding Toby's hand as we walked along the harbour with boats anchored everywhere. I was carrying a packed lunch and Toby was holding an envelope. I stopped and looked down at a boat that had sprung a leak and needed bailing out. Toby looked at it then at me; a straight line creased his little forehead while he was wondering.

'Is this okay or would you rather go on that one?' I asked him, pointing at a 40-foot speedboat. He beamed a huge smile.

'Oh, that one!'

We were on a flashy Sunseeker Predator, the kind of boat that you could live the rest of your life on. It was just Toby, who wore a sun hat with golden curls spilling out from under it, the skipper and me. We were ten miles out and Malta was just a speck of land on the horizon. As the gentle swell lifted the boat up and down, the island was visible one second and invisible the next.

The twin engines that had blasted us out here were taking a breather. We were drifting on a gentle sea and fishing for nothing in particular. Any fish, even a little tiddler, would do. People went fishing for many reasons. Fishing was just one of them. You could lose yourself out there just staring into a bottomless ocean.

'Papa, how do I know if I've hooked a fish?'

'Watch the red float. If it pops down under the surface, you may have something. You'll feel it on the line. Then give it a gentle tug.'

'What if I hook a shark?'

'You'll know. Just let the rod go or I'll have to jump in and swim after you.'

'Will we see a shark?'

'Dolphins maybe. They're much friendlier.'

'Oh, nearly forgot.' He handed me his fishing rod, went below and popped back holding an envelope.

'Grandpa asked me to give you this.' I took the envelope.

'Thank you, son. I'll open it in a minute.'

'Hey skipper, can you show my lad how this boat of yours works? Like, working the radar, setting destinations, start it, stop it, reverse it? He could write something about this one day for a school essay.'

'Sure.' I watched closely as he showed Toby the ropes. It crossed my mind that this boat would make a very good means of escaping from the island permanently.

The sun dazzled on the water, creating a shimmering sea of glittering diamonds. Toby's eyelids were batting, trying to keep focused on the red fishing float, but sleep called and he was gone. I picked him up and laid him down on the cushions under the canvas awnings, which protecting us from the midday sun. A bit of Papa was deep inside me. He used to look after me like this. He didn't have a boat like this, but he sure had a compass. Surrounded by the elements, I had a moment of calm and contentment. I closed my eyes and drifted with the ocean.

I remembered reading something in prison by Steven Spielberg that had struck home. He had written for a journal before his career went skywards. 'Between the ages of 30 and 40, you will drink excessively, experiment with drugs and disappoint a lot of people, mostly family. These years will be a blur and you won't know what happened to you.' That summed me up. I was doing all that, and my blur was such that I didn't see or comprehend it, but that was no excuse. Not all men were like that. Only at moments like this, the moments that mattered, could I see or feel anything that made the slightest scrap of sense. On the envelope, written in a child's scratchy handwriting, were the words OPEN ON THE DAY BEFORE YOUR BATTLE.

I opened the envelope carefully with my finger and thumb, not wanting to spoil its contents. Inside, neatly taped together, was the card signed by 20 boxers that Papa had handed me when I was in Hairmyres Hospital after my attack. I'd ripped the card up when I was in a rage during morphine withdrawal. I thought the pieces had been thrown away. Just a tiny scrap of card was missing, otherwise it was perfect. The missing piece somehow made it more flawless: a tiny chink in the armour, a cat with three legs. Who rescued it and who gave it to me was all that counted.

Toby stirred and stretched like a cat, just like his mother waking, with the same angularity and sequence. He was definitely his mother.

'Did we catch a fish?' he asked, still yawning and rubbing his eyes.

'Yeah, but I let it go.'

'Why?'

'He had to get back to his family.'

I asked the skipper if we could make a high-speed detour and hit Gozo for a swim before heading home. He checked his watch and pressed two buttons. The engines roared to life like angry female lions defending their territory against hyenas, and we were gone. We stopped at Mgarr. 'This is Pearl Harbour. Perfect water; cleaner than clean. Look, you can see all the way to the bottom,' the skipper said.

All three of us stripped off and jumped in. The sea water wasn't cold, and it was buoyant. There was as much salt as history in this sea. Toby could swim like a fish and I could thank his mother for making that happen. We got back on the boat, dried off, opened a packet of crisps, snapped some Cokes and headed for home. Sunseekers moved at a speed that defied logic. Toby had his hands on the wheel and was in charge for a while.

'Want some music?' shouted the skipper.

'What?' He throttled back, and the engines slowed to a rumbling, soft purr.

'There is a sound system on this boat that, when full on, is illegal unless we're ten miles out from land.'

'Illegal?' I smiled.

'Yeah, I have a finale for you. Are you ready?'

'Are you ready?' I asked Toby. He smiled and nodded.

'Okay skip, hit it!' He pressed a button and Toby pressed his hands to his ears.

'Wow!' Toby yelled as 'We Are The Champions' by Queen thundered out of the six custom-built Bose speakers. No wonder the sound system had to be played ten miles out. You could've rocked Wembley Stadium with this. All three of us started singing our hearts out. I actually started crying with the exhilaration of the moment. Toby didn't know the words like I did, but he was right in the slipstream.

The song and the engines competing for audio dominance. One second it was the song, then the big howling engines swamped the music. Malta was accelerating towards us at what felt like warp speed. The skipper turned down the music and eased back on the gas. He looked at me.

'I put a bet on you today.'

'Thank you, pal,' I said, handing him €50.

'Oh, no need.'

'Take it, skip. Today was worth a thousand times that. I owe you. Tell me, how much gas does this boat take?'

'11,000 litres.'

'What's that in miles?'

'About 3,000 cruising. Less flat out, obviously. Quite a bit more at ten or so knots. It's always full of juice because the owner insists on it. Petrol goes up in price every day. Why do you ask?'

'Just wondered. What's it worth?'

'Three and a half million, maybe more.' We got back to St Julian's harbour, gliding on a scarlet sea as the sun kissed the horizon goodnight. Toby, like the day, was dropping.

It was the best day of my life. Nothing will ever top it, not even a victory against the odds. That was all meaningless compared to a father and son sharing a moment like we just had. Out on the ocean, nobody could reach us. It was our time, and we'd gone fishing like fellas do. Laura was standing on the harbour wall smiling. Toby walked to her, turned and waved goodbye. They got in the car and drove away. Maybe I was here for a reason after all. I was thinking clearly and honestly for once. I blamed myself for what happened between me and Laura. Whatever I may have said in the past, nothing had been her fault. I needed to point the finger at me.

I didn't see Gary at first but then I saw his yellow Jeep. The big man was fast asleep in it. I walked over, switched on the ignition and blew the horn.

'Jesus. Give over, will ya? Where you been all day?'

'Fishing.' Gary had sunk a load of money into me and this fight. He must've been at his Liverpool wits' end.

'Did you catch anything?'

'Yes.'

'Well, show me. Can we eat it?'

'I'll show you tomorrow. First, I've got the interview with John Murphy at your restaurant. Shouldn't take long, then I can call it a day.' John was waiting with his cameraman in the Meet Argentinian steakhouse restaurant, which overlooked St Julian's harbour. He just wanted to get a 'night before the fight' interview.

John: Here we are with Scott Dixon in Malta, where he is waiting for his WBU world title fight versus the champion Baker Barakat, who has flown in from Germany for the title defence. Scott, do you know much about him? Have you seen much of him?

Me: I know he's quite an experienced opponent. He's had 42 pro fights or so. He also has a kick-boxing K1 background. I believe he's won the K1 championship now, as well. He knows how to fight but I noticed he hasn't boxed outside of Germany, so far as I know. I've boxed all over the place and I may be the more experienced fighter because of it. I may be a bit more of an all-round technician at the same time.

John: So, you've had your weigh-in and you've had a good look at him. What was your impression of him on the scales?

Me: When you get to the weigh-in, you look at your opponent and can half-tell how the fight is going to go. That's always a fighter's first impression. You get to size someone up and eyeball them.

John: Yeah…

Me: And I look at the guy and I see nothing that scares me, nothing that worries me. The main thing is that I've done my work in the gym and I believe that tomorrow night I'm going to be victorious over Baker Barakat.

John: You're well known over in the UK and have had some high-profile fights over the years at light-middleweight, but now you're a fully fledged super-middleweight. What do you feel is the difference? Did moving up cause you any problems?

Me: Well listen, I lived the good life for a few years after 2004, when I had my last profile fight against Matt Macklin. I kinda relaxed a bit and allowed the time needed to move up to super-middleweight. I feel nice and strong. I feel much settled. I think as you get older as well, because I'm 35 now, I've learnt to economise more on my movement and output. I can punch maybe five times harder now than I did before.

John: So, you've been out here for a number of years and you're the Maltese home fighter, yes? You're flying their flag.

Me: I've been here for seven years now. Malta is my home. I believe I'm the pride of the boxing scene over here. Boxing wasn't so dominant seven years ago when I arrived but we're on the up now, so we've got something to shout about and show people. Hopefully, tomorrow night, I'll become world champion representing Malta, which is good for the island and good for me. Yes, I'll be waving the flag.

John: And, hopefully, plenty more fights back in Malta to build up the scene on the back of seeing you win that WBU title.

Me: Malta's going to be the new hotbed of boxing and the new place to be. You have Marbella, Lanzarote and Tenerife training camps. Malta's going to be the next hotspot. And it does get pretty hot here.

John: What do you think Malta has got over other well-established places?

Me: It's just a new destination. Like a new kid on the block. And it's part of the EU now, so it's easy to do business with certain countries in terms of bringing fighters in and organising contracts. We have a promising boxing team here as well, with a lot to show the world.

John: Thanks very much for talking to us and good luck tomorrow night. I'll be watching.

Me: Thank you and God bless.

After the interview, Gary pitched up with some news. 'Got this emailed from the *Daily Record* to give you. You must have a pal at that newspaper. I dunno why they bother. Emigrated to Malta for a quiet life? You must be fucking joking. You're a nightmare.'

> Boxer Scott Dixon has been shot, stabbed, abducted and contemplated suicide. But tomorrow, he is looking to complete a remarkable comeback by becoming a world champion. It comes eight years after he was brutally beaten by a former school pal over a woman and lef with two broken legs and a broken arm.
>
> The Hamilton fighter thought about ending it all as he learned to walk again. After retiring, he emigrated to Malta in 2006 for a peaceful life, and then he rediscovered his love of boxing. Now Dixon – who was Brad Pitt's body double in *Snatch* – has a shock WBU super-middleweight shot against champ Baker Barakat in Malta.
>
> Yesterday, he said, 'It's already a great comeback. I am going to do this after all I have been through. After all the strife and the hardship, this is going to be nothing. I am just glad I am still here to tell the tale and have this opportunity to have a fight like this.'
>
> Dixon – who first boxed aged eight – became famous for his Superman shorts. He won a WBU International

title and retired as undefeated Commonwealth welterweight champ in 2000 aiming to claim the light-middleweight belt.

But Dixon fell to the 11th defeat of a 41-fight pro career a month before he was kidnapped. He finds it hard to even talk about the attack which left him unable to walk for 18 months. The 35-year-old explained, 'I retired in 2004 after being stabbed three times and shot twice. I was smashed with a baseball bat, abducted from my house and left for dead in the countryside. That was my career over. It took me about a year and a half before I could walk again.'

I got an early night and just before falling asleep, I wondered if I would ever get off the island. My dreams bought the movie rights of my thinking. Papa and I were walking slowly along the harbour pathway, reminiscing about life back home in Scotland and remembering old friends. We were just about to cross the road when a white Ford Transit van came careering down the middle of the road. A man in the passenger seat fired two shots, and a young woman who was walking her Alsatian puppy fell dead on the pavement. Papa took a bullet intended for me, then Gran flew over and told me I had to change my ways. With the help of the Kiwi Sean, who made bombs and lived in a secluded place on the north side of the island, I decided to blow up a government building, along with a penthouse flat in the silent city. I then stole the Sunseeker, set course for North Africa and slipped out during the chaos under a quarter-moon wearing night-vision goggles.

When I woke up in a sweat, that was all I could remember. I definitely wanted to get off the island, but it would be as though I was running away from a fight. I rang Papa.

'You okay, Papa?'

'Yes. You all set? It's a big day.' It was just a dream.

Round 12

Now or Never

25 August 2012

We had planned to hold the match on Malta's national football pitch, but it had just been laid with Astroturf, costing 250,000 Euros, and we never got approval because of it. The crowd could damage it with chair legs and cigarettes and what have you. So, we held it next door on the training pitch. It still had all the floodlights we needed. The arena had a historical military building that the Brits had built, and it was a fantastic, eye-catching backdrop for the fight.

I'd left all the organisational details for Gary to sort out. For one reason or another, he thought I'd do some of it while training my balls off.

Turned out, Gary forgot about the round cards for the ring girls, as well as a bucket for me to spit in. Fifteen minutes before the fight, four little honeys, one of which I was seeing on and off, came into the changing room to get the cards we didn't have. Gary told them to get out and I snapped. 'What are you doing? Who the hell are you to talk like that?'

The room went quiet. Papa couldn't believe what he was seeing and hearing. Any second now, my manager and I were going to be at each other like cat and dog. Fortunately, all that calmed down and paled into insignificance, which is what it was, because we got presented with a much bigger problem nobody could've anticipated.

Barakat's manager wanted payment there and then, before the fight, or they were walking out. I was ready to fight, all set to go and pumped up, and now we were dealing with all this palaver. I hadn't bet on myself, which was just as well. It was against the odds and I didn't need the bollocks and distraction. Gary stepped in.

'I don't know if you can read but that's not the arrangement we agreed. I don't have the money, not yet, as you know.'

'Okay then. We're not fighting,' Barakat's manager said. This was ten minutes before the fight.

I went and grabbed our co-promoter Steve Collins and filled him in. 'They want payment now or no fight. That's total bollocks. It's not how it works. The contract is with the WBU, and they look after all that,' I relayed.

'Right,' said Steve, following me back to where I had left Barakat's manager. Steve sized him up. 'Look, I've been in the business most of my life. The contract is between the promotion and the WBU. My boy's gonna be in the ring in five minutes. If your fella isn't, you forfeit the fight and give us the belt. Am I being clear enough? If not, I'll say it again.' Barakat's manager left us and came back two minutes later.

'I'm not happy about this but okay, we'll fight. We'll sort all this out later.' Steve didn't respond. There was nothing to say or sort out.

There is something in a boxer you can't find in other kinds of men. In most cases, they're not just fighting their opponent. They're fighting to get out of the slums, for a better life, as well as recognition, self-worth and respect. It was a battle all right. Nobody likes or wants a loser for long. If there's magic in boxing, it's the realisation of understanding a dream that nobody saw but you.

Being prepared and ring-ready was everything. I always went in warmed up, limbered up, loose and already sweating. If you went in cold, you'd come out cold. Even if you were boxing your best pal, he was your worst enemy for 36 minutes. Most fighters did have respect for one other, no matter what the papers said.

Most of the pre-fight, face-to-face stuff was just to ramp up the fans and get media attention. Occasionally, genuine hostility broke loose at the weigh-ins or the interviews, but that was rare. Nobody liked it and it was bad for the sport. I was ready for Barakat, but he was a tricky customer with a good right. He was nicknamed Doctor Liver because of his accurate body shots and I took nothing away from him. His belt, though? I could take that. It had been a long time since I'd fought at this level, but my head was ready. I needed my body to catch up before we kicked off.

Since coming to Malta seven years ago, this wasn't a fight I believed would happen. There had just been too many obstacles, and I still wasn't firing on all cylinders. My ankle told me this was going to be an uphill battle, while the plate in my arm reminded me that I was anything but armour-plated. When I managed to crawl for help after the attack on my life, I realised something important, though: if my heart was in it, there was nothing I couldn't do.

Fortunately, my heart was in this. This was something in my life I had always wanted. I had battled for it, struggled for it and prayed for it. I just wanted to be somebody, even if it was only for a day. The real motivation wasn't about fame or glory. It was about repaying my Papa for all of his work, patience, direction and faith in me. After all that he had done for me, I wanted to hand him the belt. He deserved it.

If I could rewind my life and delete the coke, booze, madness, violence and crime, I might've won this title years ago, but I'd never know. I *did* know that when I won, the boxing world would be taken by surprise. I would've preferred to go into the ring thinking I had nothing to lose, but that mindset doesn't work, and it wasn't true. I went into the ring to win the belt. I did have something to lose.

We used the football pitch changing rooms as dressing rooms, so we had to walk across the football field to get to the ring. I held the Maltese flag high as I walked across the field, while Papa, Ludwig and Jap Kavanagh walked alongside me. My Superman theme music kicked in, which hyped me up, so I started running towards the ring, igniting the crowd.

I needed to keep my body temperature up and the weather helped. It must've been 25°C that night.

I gave Papa a kiss on the forehead, as always, and vaulted into the ring. I kept moving, stabbing and rotating my head like Tyson. Barakat made his entrance. He's Syrian, so they played some wailing, Egyptian-sounding music that the crowd seemed to like. He came in very slowly and it took about five minutes for him to get into the ring. The MC introduced me first then Barakat, informing the crowd it was Barakat's fifth title defence. 'Set the table before you eat,' Papa whispered in my ear. 'Get it laid out neat and tidy. Don't get involved too early, bide your time.'

The MC agreed to announce each round because we had no cards. What a shambles. I still couldn't get over it – a world title fight with no cards. It was like *Monty Python*, just fucking mad. Maybe I should've been fighting stark-bollock naked, wearing only Steve Aquilina's filthy socks. I always had strange thoughts before and during fights. I think humour helped me to stay focused in a weird way. Steve's probably wearing them now, I thought.

The MC was well up for this and he announced the fight well. I was always impressed by the way boxing announcers could raise their voices and boom out words in an upward, curving crescendo type of way. 'Round ... one!' By the look on his face, I figured he was enjoying it. It wasn't every day that the MC was asked to shout out the rounds. Assuredly, the crowd would've preferred looking up the skirts of pretty ring girls. I know I would've, but this was what we had.

During the first round, I landed a few peachy body shots and a few good lefts. Barakat was 5ft 8in and I was 6ft even. Some say that was the height of Jesus, but who knows? My reach was better but pound-for-pound, he could hit harder. I also had good control of the ring centre. The centre was the place to be, unless you could pin the other guy on the ropes. The ring centre gave you the whole space to work and operate in. Ringmasters, the greats, knew this space well. 'Operating at max potential from the centre meant you ran the show,' I'd heard someone say one time.

In round two, Barakat came out like a bull. I boxed on the back foot, jabbed and stabbed, looking for openings. My jab was working. I was showing him, then cracking him. I then changed my stance, going both ways fast, checking to see if he could keep up. Ten seconds before the bell, he caught me with a couple and I felt them. No question, he could punch.

As round three started, I thought I was in front, but it was probably closer to even. The crowd was yelling now, raising the tempo and supporting their adopted Maltese boy. Toby was in the front row and I heard him yell, 'Knock him out, Daddy.' I landed some big punches, turning Barakat's head one way then another. I was also covering up well, receiving no damage to worry me. Then he caught me, behind my right elbow, right-bang in the liver – a prescription from the Doctor. I brought my gloves up to cover my face. I didn't want him to see I was out of breath from the punch. He made a business out of hammering livers and had just pounded the life out of mine.

The fourth round didn't prove anything but in the fifth round, I started to take his title away. I won the fifth, no doubt about it, then in the sixth Barakat came out looking like a guy who'd found something. I wasn't sure what that 'something' may have been but I got him in the corner, launched a perfect right uppercut, then connected with a solid left hook. He was now swaying. A boxer has a switch, like an overdrive they flip on when it's time to close a fight. I flipped the switch and started throwing single, hard punches. He kept staggering without throwing anything back.

I started thinking in millionths of seconds. If this was a 12-round fight, we were halfway through it, so there would be a long time to go if he stayed on his feet. So, if I let it all rip now and he survived, then I may run out of steam later, which had happened before. I had all my skills and plans stirring in one big pot of multiple fight scenarios. I needed to pick out what I needed when I was positive I needed them, so ultimately decided to turn my overdrive switch back off.

In the seventh, I started to feel the fight, so I became more cautious and slowed it down. Papa's voice was in my head. 'If you feel tired and the punches are coming in, ride the punches,' he'd say. Some refer to this as 'riding the bike', which means that instead of staying upright, you ride into the punches and box off the jab.

In round eight, the fight was getting heavy but still manageable. I took a swinging shot that got me bang on the ear. Suddenly, the crowd sounded hollow, distant and echoing. When I got back to my corner, I couldn't hear anything much out of the ear. From what I could hear, Papa said, 'Stick to the game plan, you're gonna be okay,' while Steve Collins added, 'Just box and box,' which wasn't a lot of help.

In the last round, I was feeling cocky. I must've found an energy reserve and was throwing good, fast-shot combinations – pa-pa, pa-pa – then moving off and letting him come at me while making him miss. We grappled, then I pushed him on to the canvas. No boxer liked being on the canvas, no matter what caused it. As he got up, I dropped my hands to bait him to come at me. I caught him solid on the way in, and he reeled backwards into the ropes. If the ropes hadn't been there, he would've been in the crowd. The final bell sounded to end it.

I dropped to my knees and put my head in my hands. I knew I'd done it, at last. Papa calculated I was seven rounds clear before we'd started the 12th. If I was or wasn't, the last round was definitely mine by a mile. It always takes time for scorecards to be collected but this time it seemed to take longer than usual. By then, the ring was full of people all waiting for the MC to announce the result.

'Ladies and gentlemen, we have a split decision.' My heart sank. I'd got this far against all the odds. Not another blow, surely? 'Judge Jan Teleki scores 116-112, Judge Benny Decroos, 116-112, and Judge Mustafa Erenay, 115-113.' I took a deep breath. 'And the new super-middleweight champion of the world ... Super Scott Dixon!'

Fireworks lit up the night sky, but the celebration wasn't for me. In Malta, there was a religious festival being held seemingly every day, and today was no exception. But that was okay. I didn't need fireworks. Papa wore a smile that shone like a beacon in the ring and in my heart. I hadn't seen him smile like that for years. Gary told me later that when the decision was announced, Papa turned to the crowds and put his arms up like the superstar he was but never took credit for.

After 12 rounds, there was nothing left in my energy bucket. I was drained and there was still a way to go before the night was over. They put the belt around me and took photographs. After the photos, I took the belt off and handed it to Papa.

'It's yours Papa, not mine.' He handed it back to me.

'It takes real guts to do what you've done. It's yours, and you've earned it in spite of everything. That's all in the past. I'm proud of you, son. I don't know where you get it from.'

'Yes, you do,' I replied. He smiled, which was worth more than any belt.

After the fight, I was ready for home, but we had a press conference first. We all sat down at a table below the ring and Ritchie Kinsella, who we'd asked to help out, kicked it off. He spoke the kind of phonetic language that English-speaking people could understand. Along with my Scottish accent, Gary was so Liverpudlian that nobody understood a word he said.

'Well, that was an absolutely brilliant performance with great body punching. It was a monumental comeback for Super Scott Dixon, who is on top of the world again. Sitting to my left is a fella who comes about 65 miles from where I was brought up, and he wants to say a few words on behalf of Malta boxing. Here he is … the former undefeated WBO world middleweight and undefeated super-middleweight champion of the world, ladies and gentlemen, the one and only, Mr Steve Collins!'

Steve took over. He was always great with words. He could talk all night, like so many Irish people. Steve had a lot to do with not only making the night a success, but making the match happen at all. 'I want to thank the people here tonight who supported us and made this happen. Gary Hincks and Michael Bennett, who worked hard, Toby Dixon, of course, and coach Ludwig Muscat. For all of us, it was very important that Scott won tonight. Deep in our hearts, we knew he had the ability and he proved it. I also want to thank the WBU officials for coming over here. What we have witnessed, now that Scott has brought home the world title to Malta, is a new future for Maltese boxing.

'We will be launching a new initiative called Malta Nights Boxing Promotion. Malta has a lot of gifted and talented young boxers, and we want to promote these quality Maltese fights. With our good connections in America, the UK, Ireland and Germany, it's going to happen. Congratulations to everybody, one and all. And to one person in particular, Super Scott Dixon! This was your night!' Steve had managed to get the words 'Malta' and 'Maltese' in his speech so many times, you'd have thought he was Maltese and not Irish. But it was a knockout speech and just what Malta and the rest of the world needed to hear.

During the press conference, I was totally drained of energy. I'd taken a few big punches, my ankle was killing me, and I couldn't really hear much. At the time, I just wished everyone would evaporate but Ritchie, my spokesperson, wanted me to talk about the fight. Everything was fuzzy, and I couldn't think straight. I nudged Steve. 'Can we hurry this up?' I asked. Steve looked at me and weighed me up in a flash. I could see he knew what I was going through.

'Keep it short and we're out of here, Scott.' Steve nodded to Ritchie.

'And now, we're going to pass you over to the new super-middleweight champion of the world. Ladies and gentlemen, Malta's adopted son, Super Scott Dixon,' announced Ritchie while handing me the mic. I wasn't sure if I could string two words together without sounding like a babbling brook. My mind was closing in on me.

What it had taken to get to this moment was costing me more than I had to give. I'd won something that people would now queue up to take from me. I was either going to need to prepare to do this again or quit. My mind started spinning. Why had Papa always stuck by my side? Why did Gary give a shit at all? How did some of my friends become like brothers? I was an okay boxer but not *that* good. Did I deserve any of this? On the day of reckoning, if I was lucky enough to get to the gates, there would be some explaining to do. Please let me in. I beg you. Please don't send me back where I came from. I can't go through that twice.

'Thank you very much. I'd just like to thank everybody for supporting me, especially everyone with me tonight, who've been with me after all these years. To make a comeback after my attack and win a title, especially here in Malta, my new home, is absolutely fantastic. We have great prospects on the way up and we're going to enjoy some big fights here in Malta. I am sure of that. With Steve on board and Team Dixon, we're going to go places … I'm gonna hand you back to …'

I couldn't remember Ritchie's name. I tried to say it three times but I'm not sure if I could've remembered my own name at that moment. Ritchie turned to me and spoke quietly into the one ear I could hear out of. 'Scott, you okay? You need a checking-over or maybe a scan?'

'Let's get this over first,' I said, handing the mic to Ritchie.

'Okay, again, I would like to say "thank you" to everybody on Scott's team. They know who they are. And we'd also like to thank all the Maltese who are here tonight and obviously the WBU boys. Without Malta's participation and support, Scott and the German boys wouldn't be here. I think Scott has done the job tonight for Maltese boxing. This is going to kick off in a big way and we would like your support in the future. So, again, thank you very much, everybody.'

The pain in my ankle was beyond my threshold. Gary knew me backwards, so he knew what was happening. The paramedics arrived, checked me over, and the boys carried me across the football pitch to the changing room. I was drained. After the crowd left the arena, Gary had to organise clearing it up, so Laura came with me to the Black Bull for a few drinks. At the time, it was the last place I wanted to go, with the last person I wanted to go with. I would've been much happier sitting with Papa saying nothing, but he'd taken Toby home.

Laura was a complication I didn't want. Because I'd won, maybe she sniffed money. I didn't know for sure but sensed this could've been the case. I craved sleep like a drug addict that hadn't had a fix in days. Tonight, my curfew was extended, which had taken some negotiation. If I didn't make curfew, there would be more problems and maybe even more prison. At the Black Bull, with my guard not only down, but gone, Laura began banging on at me, offloading about what I'd done to her. The words were going in one ear and straight out of the other. I started to wish that both of my eardrums had been damaged.

In the morning, after a night of sleeping and waking, checking the situation and absorbing what had happened the night before, I tapped Laura gently on her shoulder to wake her. She stirred and opened her eyes. 'Hey, I'm sorry. I can't do this any more,' I said. 'I'll do my best to look after you both. Don't say a word, please.'

I wanted to meet up with Papa, just him and me. I didn't want an audience. Over the years, I must've been a real disappointment to him. I had no doubt about that. Papa could've easily lost faith in my boxing skills. More importantly, he could've lost faith in me because of some of my questionable life decisions, but he'd never once nailed me or lost faith. Maybe it would've been better for everyone if he had nailed me at times, since he was the only person I had ever really listened to.

I sat down on a stone wall, which overlooked where St Julian's harbour stopped and the open sea began. For the first time in my life, I was blind to all the women sunbathing in bikinis. Instead, I kept looking over my shoulder for Papa. I sprawled out on the uncomfortable stone wall, as lumpy and hard as a prison mattress, and closed my eyes. I must've drifted off. I opened them to a blinding midday sun, rose from the stone wall with the speed of a first sit-up and turned around.

Passing Julio's Restaurant, about 300 yards behind me, I saw a man with long, flowing white hair walking as fast and spry as a teenager. He didn't walk like an old man. He walked like a man with life and spirit deep in his bones. Some men die long before they're put into the ground. Not him – ever. At that moment, I couldn't imagine my life without Papa. Before the fight, I thanked God that Papa was alive to share the moment. Even if I had lost, I would've known that I had given it a decent shot as a professional fighter again. Papa had never approved of me fighting unlicensed. 'That's the beginning of the end,' he would say. 'Prove me otherwise or be a taxi driver.'

Walking towards me in the midday sunshine was the man in my life. I figured the only reason he was late was because he'd been with Toby. I would've staked my belt on it. I thought about Toby forming a relationship with Papa, who my son shared a name with, and the thought of their bond overwhelmed me.

It was never really the words that Papa had said that bone-deep affected me, although his words were important. Many times, Papa's words echoed in my mind, helping to form my moral conscience. More so, it was what Papa didn't say – his thoughts behind his eyes and his demeanour that reflected his spirit. With him, silence was a very powerful thing. In that silence, I was forced to fire my thoughts straight back at myself in the hope of finding an answer. I always knew what Papa wanted for me, so he never really had to say it. But I needed to express what I wanted for him and Gran. Maybe more importantly, it had been too long since I had simply said 'thank you'. It had been even longer since I had said 'I love you'.

On the way to meet Papa, I had popped into church for a few moments of silence and to send a message upstairs. Over the years, if I hadn't gone to church, I wouldn't have had any place to go when things unravelled. While there, I admitted to myself that I should go to church more often when things were ravelled and good.

I walked towards Papa, matching the pace he'd set. He beamed me a big smile, similar to the one I'd seen last night. That type of smile from Papa was a rare but life-affirming sight. 'Well, son, what a night! Let's take this moment together while we can,' he said as we met. We then walked without speaking towards the place I'd been resting. We sat down in unison on a bench and he turned to me. I could tell he was excited.

'What you achieved last night, Scott, was the stuff of dreams. It takes a special kind of man, with guts and something else from deep inside, to do that. You've never, for a moment, been without my love but last night was something, son. To be honest, my heart was in my mouth while we waited for the result. I hope you've called your grandmother.' He took a deep breath.

'Yes, I called Gran. But, Papa, I wanted … I needed … to win for you.' He looked at me and thought about what I'd said.

'Scott, but son, I wanted the win for you,' he said quietly.

We then sat without speaking for half an hour. Maybe people walked past us or maybe they didn't. Maybe the sun had set or maybe it was another day entirely. Perhaps, we weren't even here at all. After a while, another familiar voice started to speak to me. What if your grandfather is ill? He won't live forever. What if he dies in Scotland? Will the authorities allow you to leave? Surely, they'd let me leave, wouldn't they? What about your grandmother? How does she *really* fit into the great and wily scheme of things?

I was thinking too much, which sometimes could distract, but that voice had saved my life before. What was its agenda? In this exact moment, what should I say or do?

Papa broke the silence. 'You'll need to do whatever you do next with care, Scott. Don't rush at it. If you must, pick off a few title challengers but go at your own pace. You're in charge now, at least for a while. Success is short lived, and nothing lasts forever. You know that.'

'Is there anything else, Papa? I'm listening loud and clear out of my one good ear,' I laughed. 'I think the other one might be perforated.' We looked into each other eyes without blinking. I knew what he was going to say. He stroked his prominent chin, which needed shaving, and looked me straight in my eyes.

'When it all sinks in, Scott, you could try taking another shot at life.'